Going Pro for $200

&

How to Choose a Prime Lens

Shawn M. Tomlinson's
Guide to Photography
Volumes 5 & 6

by

shawn m tomlinson

2015

Going Pro for $200 & How to Choose a Prime Lens

Shawn M. Tomlinson's
Guide to Photography
Volumes 5 & 6

ISBN: 978-1-329-39645-6

Cover photo © 2014 by
Gary W. Ziroli

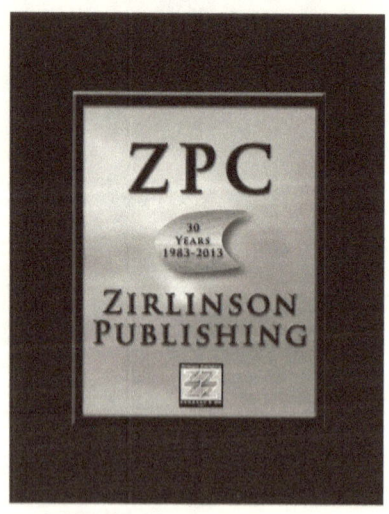

Contents

Going Pro for $200

Shawn M. Tomlinson's
Guide to Photography
Volume 5

Cover photo © 2014 by
Gary W. Ziroli

Note: The Nikon D1's aperture-priority mode is designated as "A" on the DSLR. I use "Av" for this mode throughout this guide series to prevent confusion with "Auto" mode on some cameras.

Note: The captions for the photos give the location, date and camera data for each image. What it means is:

Nikon D1, 80mm, 1/250, f/9, ISO 200, P, pattern metering
© 2014, 2015 by Shawn M. Tomlinson

Camera: Nikon D1
Focal Length: 80mm
Shutter Speed: 1/250
Aperture: f/9
ISO sensitivity: 200
Mode: P (program)
Metering: Pattern

Other Modes are:
S: shutter priority
Av: aperture priority
M: manual

Going Pro for $200

Revisiting
the
Nikon D1

Shawn M. Tomlinson's
Guide to Photography
Volume 5

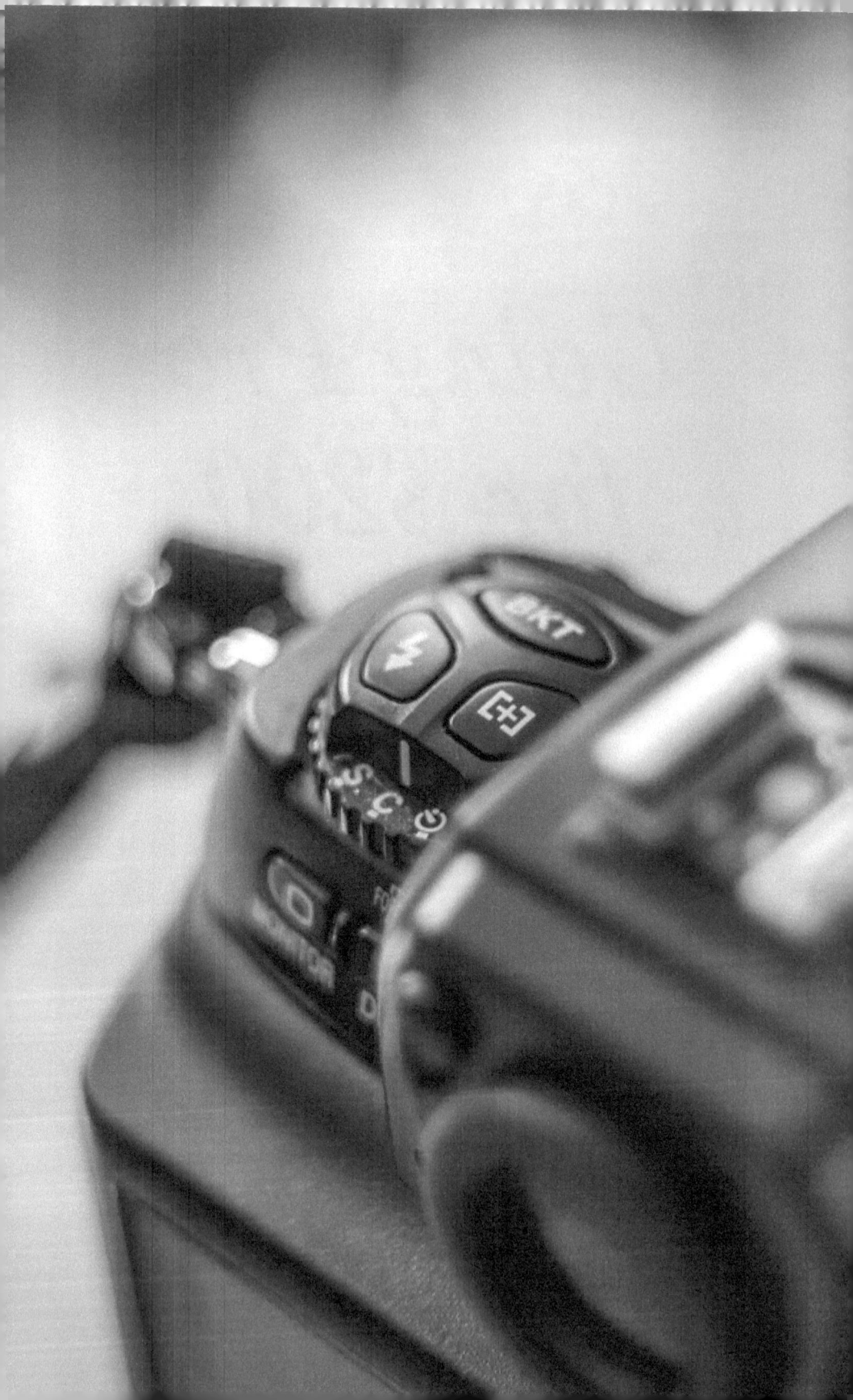

First Words

You've heard about the wonders of the professional digital single-lens reflex cameras, how they handle, how they feel in your hands.

You've looked at Internet reviews and sample images.

You've ooooed and ahhhed at every curve, button and dial on the pro DSLRs.

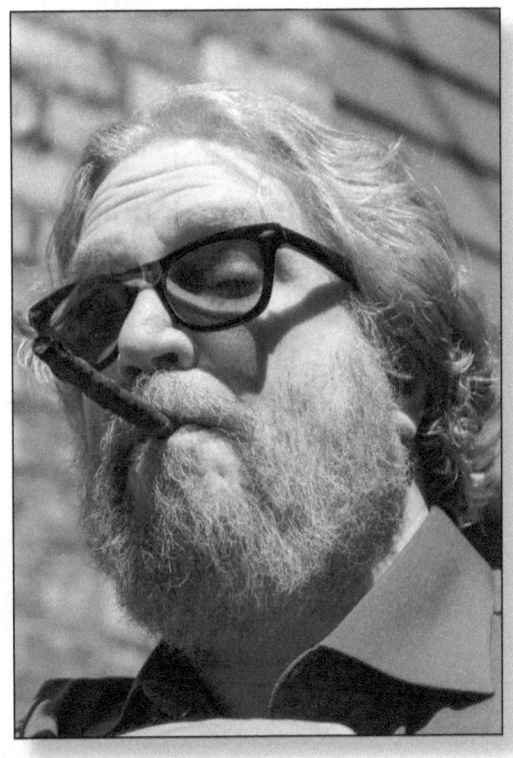

Shawn M. Tomlinson,
Saratoga Springs, NY, July 11, 2015.
© 2015 Gary W. Ziroli

Let's face it: you've drooled.

So have I.

But those prices. Yikes.

Never did you think as a photographer enthusiast or wedding photographer or weekend photographer that a pro DSLR — a Canon 1DX, a Nikon D3X or a Nikon D4S — was within reach.

The price tags on these beauties range from a mere $6,500 for the D4S to $6,800 for the 1DX and a whopping $8,000 for the D3X.

OK, well, I guess that Nikon D3300 will be nice, too, or that Canon EOS Rebel... NO! I will NOT succumb! I will not walk around carrying a DSLR that says "Rebel" on it. NEVER!

Don't worry. You don't have to, either.

In fact, you can put your hands on a professional DSLR body and a lens for around $200 if you real-

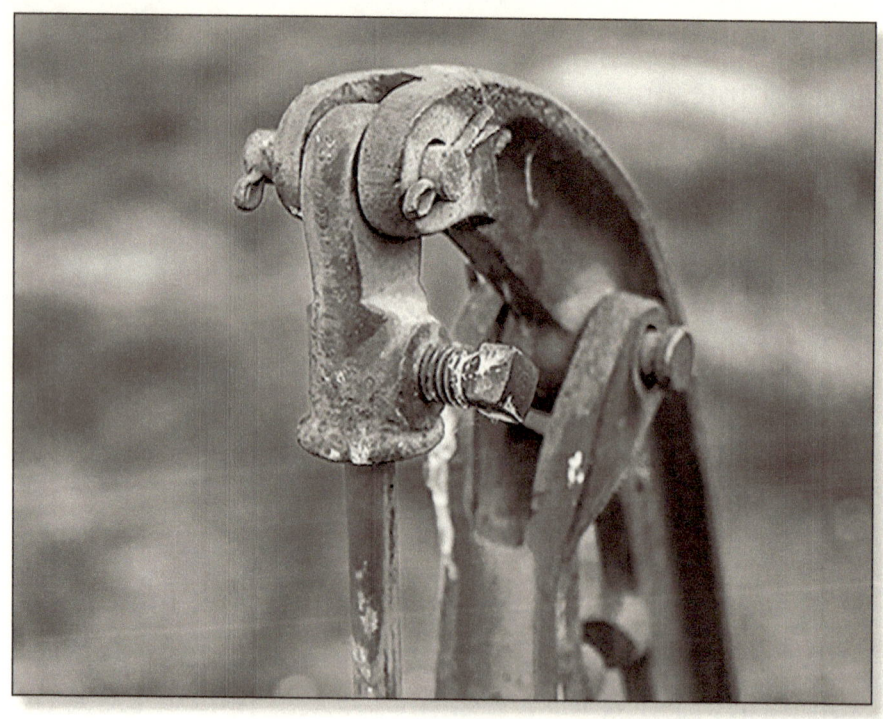

Broadalbin-Mayfield Rural Cemetery, Broadalbin, NY, June 15, 2014
Nikon D1, 52mm, 1/125, f/4.8, ISO 200, Av, pattern metering
© 2014, 2015 by Shawn M. Tomlinson

ly want to know what all the fuss is about.

No, I'm not talking about a Nikon D4S that, ah, "fell off a truck" somewhere.

I'm talking about the very first, ground-up DSLR for the professional market.

The Nikon D1.

Many may scoff, but there are good reasons to acquire this pro DSLR that once cost $6,000 when it was new in 1999. That's $8,551.01 in 2015 dollars, according to the U.S. Bureau of Labor Statistics.

The first reason is you can get one now for around $100.

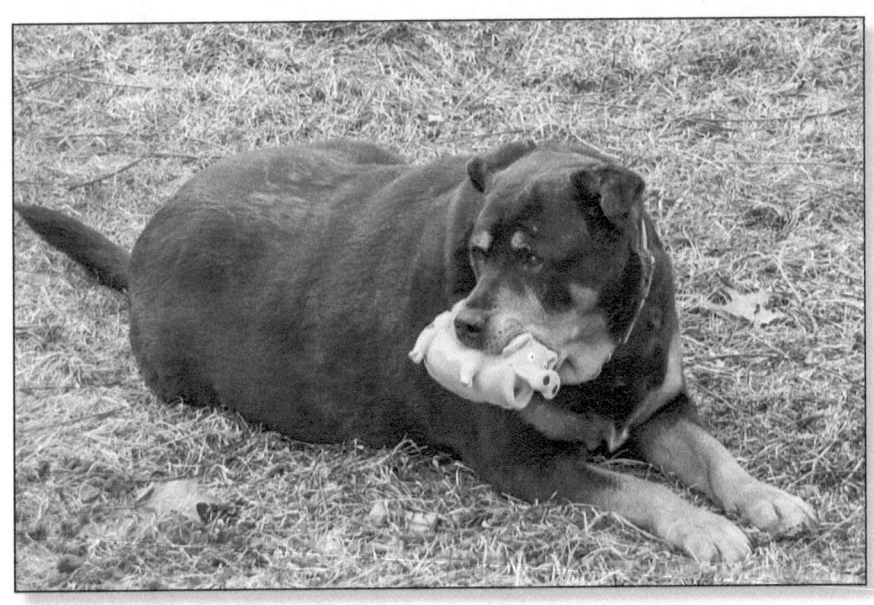

Baby, Ballston Lake, NY, Jan. 1, 2015
Nikon D1, 80mm, 1/125, f/5.6, ISO 400, Av, pattern metering
© 2015 by Shawn M. Tomlinson

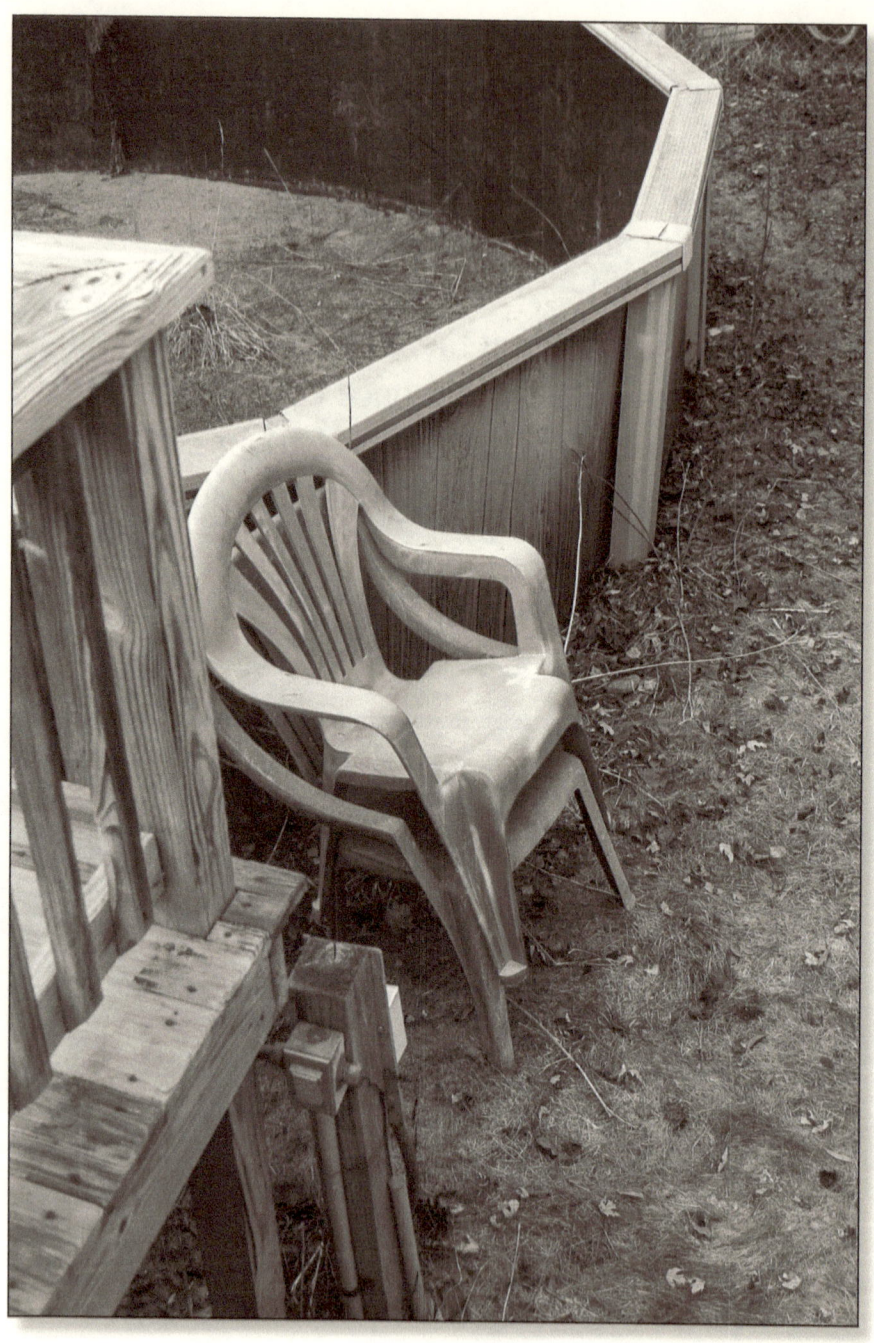

Ballston Lake, NY, Jan. 1, 2015
Nikon D1, 28mm, 1/500, f/3.5, ISO 400, Av pattern metering
© 2015 by Shawn M. Tomlinson

Part 1
The Pro 'Feel'

In the film SLR days, as now in the DSLR days, the professional cameras had a solid, study, beat-hell-out-of-it-all-day-and-it-works-fine build. They were built, at least by the 1970s, to feel good in your hands.

And they do.

The best feeling, best looking workhorse pro SLR was the Nikon F4S. Sure, the F5 still gets all

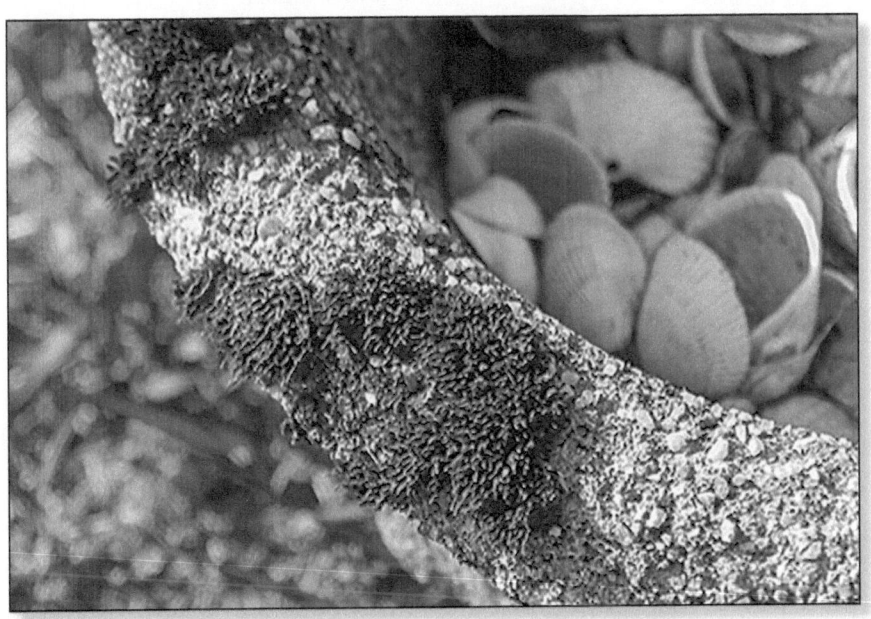

Broadalbin-Mayfield Rural Cemetery, Broadalbin, NY, June 15, 2014
Nikon D1, 82mm, 1/250, f/5.6, ISO 200, Av, pattern metering
© 2014, 2015 by Shawn M. Tomlinson

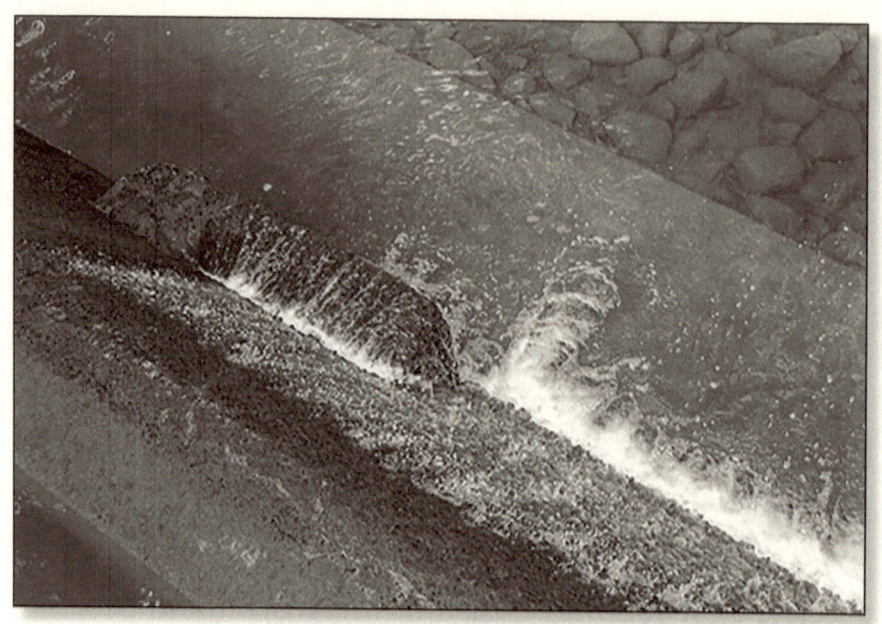

Indian Kill Nature Preserve, Glenville, NY, July 21, 2014
Nikon D1, 28mm, 1/125, f/3.5, ISO 200, Av pattern metering
© 2014, 2015 by Shawn M. Tomlinson

the accolades, but it was an uglier, heavier version of the elegant, sleek, redesigned-from-scratch-practically F4S. This film SLR, the F4S, is the closest thing to a modern DSLR you can hold that takes fantastic images on film. It looks an feels a lot like a modern pro DSLR. I like the look and feel of it so much, I often have dreamed about putting the guts of a D1 or D1x or D2x inside the F4S somehow and getting the best of both worlds.

As good as the F4S was/is, though, the photography world did not freeze frame on it for all time. Instead, Nikon went to the F5 and then starting working with Rochester's now-fallen giant, Kodak, to combine its camera bodies with Kodak's digital sensors.

After working with Kodak off and on for a few years, the fellas at Nikon decided, "screw this" and designed their first wholly original DSLR. It was the D1, the prelude to the 21st century and the turning point — at

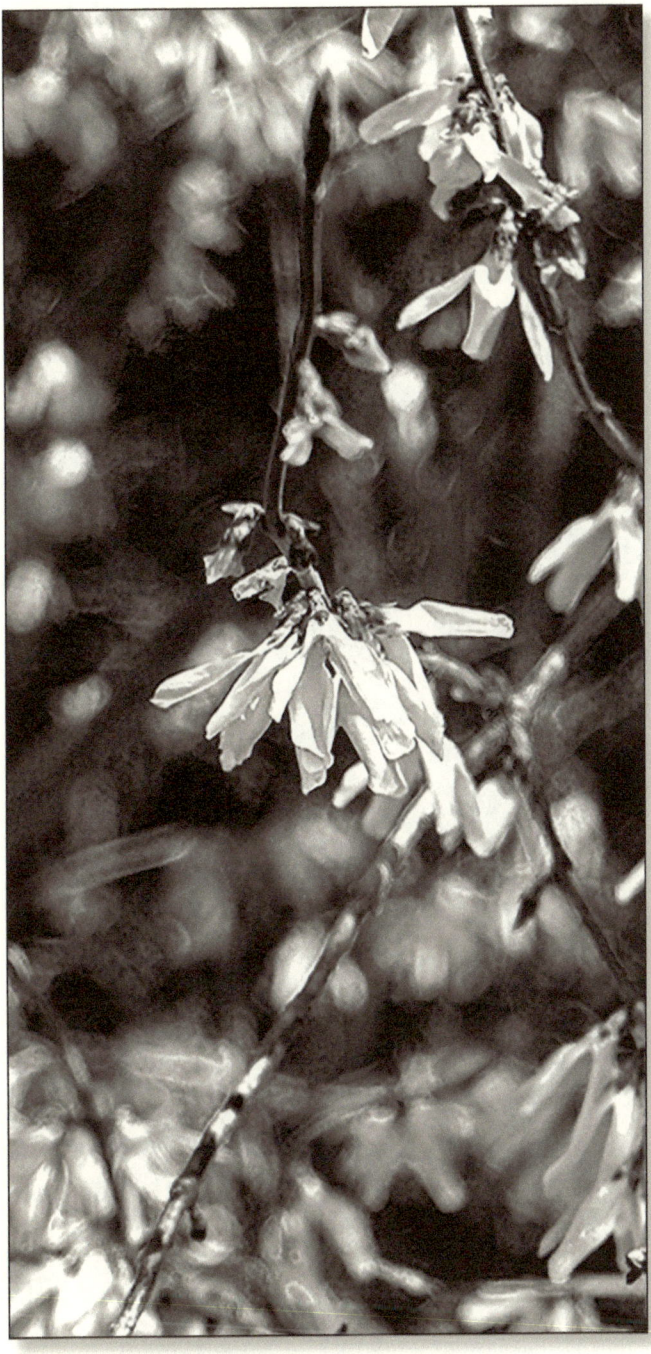

Ballston Lake, NY, May 1, 2014
Nikon D1, 66mm, 1/1500, f/5.3, ISO 200, Av, spot metering
© 2014, 2015 by Shawn M. Tomlinson

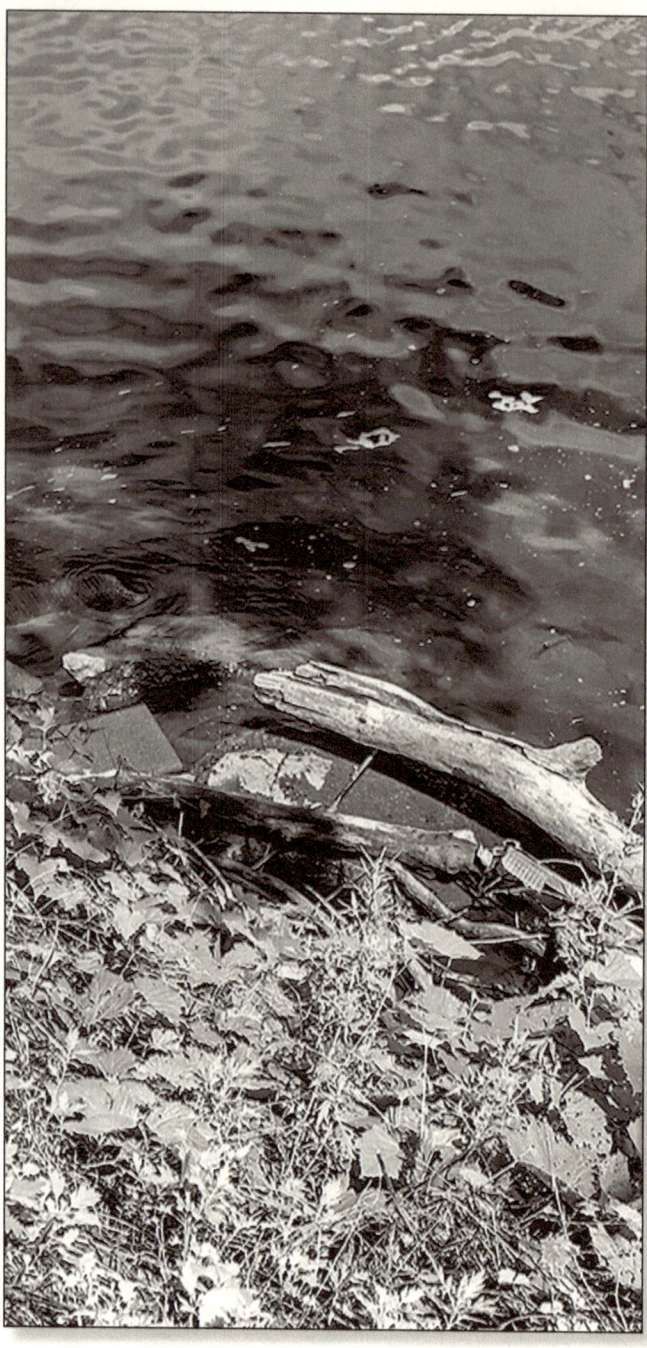

Kiwanis Park, Rotterdam Junction, NY, July 29, 2014
Nikon D1, 35mm, 1/1000, f/3.8, ISO 200, Av, pattern metering
© 2014, 2015 by Shawn M. Tomlinson

least from an historical perspective — from film to digital.

OK, it probably owes more of its design to the Nikon F5, but there is a certain elegance to it that is reminiscent of the F4S.

The differences between pro cameras and everything really is who they are built for.

Entry-level cameras are marketed to people just making the transition from point-and-shoot cameras or their smartphone cameras to the first tentative steps into serious photography. The camera makers always realized that to capture this audience, they need to make these entry-level cameras as cheap as possible while retaining the quality associated with the brand name.

Every camera manufacturer took this idea a little too far at least once each in the film era. Nikon's biggest load of crap was the EM. Canon's was the T50. Pentax joined in with several, but notably, the ZX-50.

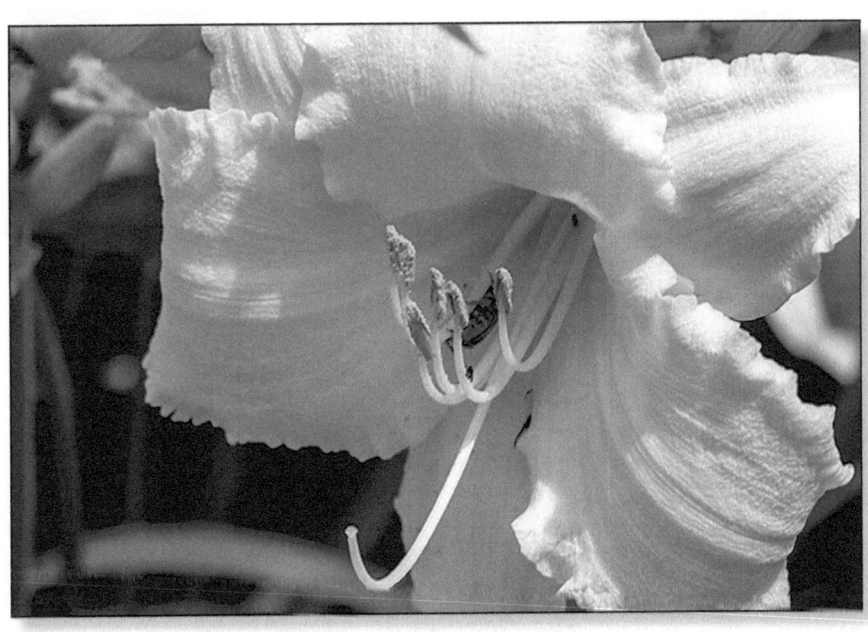

Saratoga Springs, NY, July 8, 2014
Nikon D1, 80mm, 1/250, f/9, ISO 200, P, pattern metering
© 2014, 2015 by Shawn M. Tomlinson

For those already familiar with SLR cameras, each company made mid-range models: Nikon's FE, Canon's A-1, Pentax's MX.

But the pros always got special treatment. This was and is the primary market for SLRs/DSLRs as the starting point from which the entry-level and mid-range cameras later are derived. The latest innovations are in the pro models, certainly, but it's more than that.

Professional photographers, especially those covering news and sports, tend to bang up their gear a lot. Not on purpose, of course, but in the course of "getting the shot." Pros can't be worried about handling their cameras delicately or they would be too concerned with that and not concerned enough with that important photograph.

So, from early on, pro cameras had to withstand the type of unintentional abuse that cheaper cameras did not.

This means that the inner frame of pro cameras is very tough metal. It means the outer plastic is very strong. It means hitting a pro DSLR on something while racing down the basketball court won't stop the shoot.

Picking up any pro DSLR, holding it in your hands and shooting with it is a very different experience than other DSLRs. You can feel the strength, the sturdiness. It gives you confidence and lets you know you aren't likely to be betrayed by a failing camera in the middle of an important assignment.

All DSLRs can produce fantastic images, so it's important to have the one in your hands that "feels" right, that gives you the best control over your images, and the one that serves you best as a camera.

Not everyone likes the feel of pro DSLRs, mainly because they are significantly heavier than other DSLR cameras.

Those who do just love that resounding and reassuring sound the pro shutter release makes.

Sure, there are times when smaller, semi-pro or "enthusiast" cameras make things easier. Backpacking up a mountain, for example, where every ounce counts, is not the best place for a pro DSLR. And, for the most part, pro DSLRs weren't designed for that anyway.

They were designed for speed and for durability.

That very fact means that buying an older one, even as old as the Nikon D1, raises the odds your new old pro camera still will be working, doing its job as it always did it.

And, since no one is going to use a D1 for a crucial photographic assignment more than a decade-and-a-half after it was made, it's going to be cheap.

More importantly, it's going to be fun.

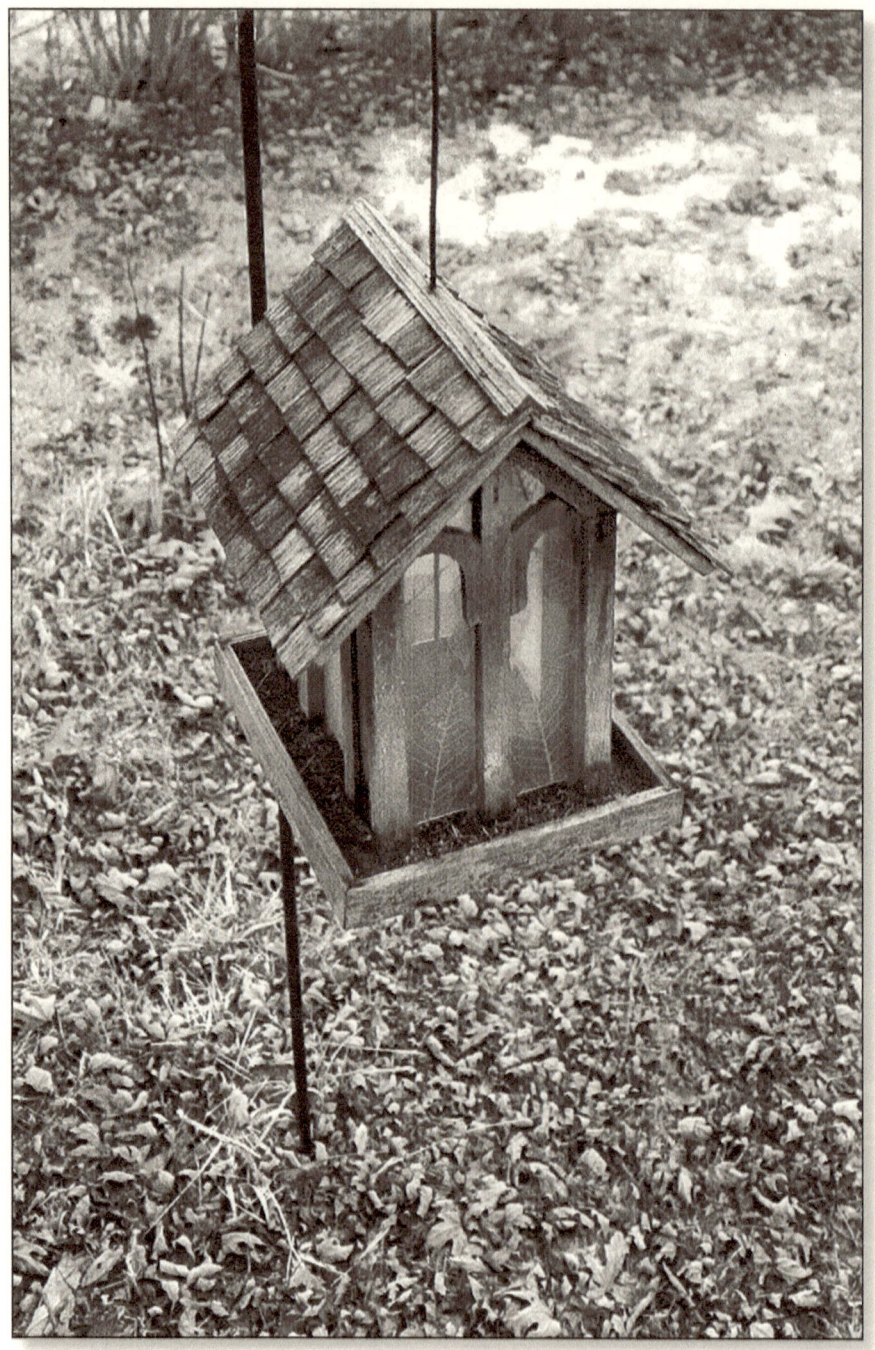

Ballston Lake, NY, Jan. 2, 2015
Nikon D1, 18mm, 1/200, f/3.5, ISO 800, M, pattern metering
© 2015, 2015 by Shawn M. Tomlinson

Part 2
The Pros and Cons of Pro DSLRs

Certainly if you're going to spend more than $6,000 for a new pro DSLR, there aren't many cons. If you want to try a pro DSLR for little money, that means buying an older one and, in this case, the Nikon D1, so there are some cons, but pros as well. Here are the basics:

Pros

- Well-built camera
- Sturdy
- CompactFlash (CF) card (sturdier than SecureDigital [SD] cards)
- Several file formats (RAW, TIFF, JPEG)
- Good color rendition
- Smaller RAW files
- Built-in battery grip
- Viewfinder blind
- Depth-of-field preview
- Vertical shutter release
- Fast, accurate focusing

- Accepts all Nikon lenses from the mid-1970s onward
- Rapid continual shooting
- VERY cheap

Cons

- Low resolution (by today's standards)
- Heavy
- Convoluted menu system
- Short battery life
- Long buffering time
- Small monitor

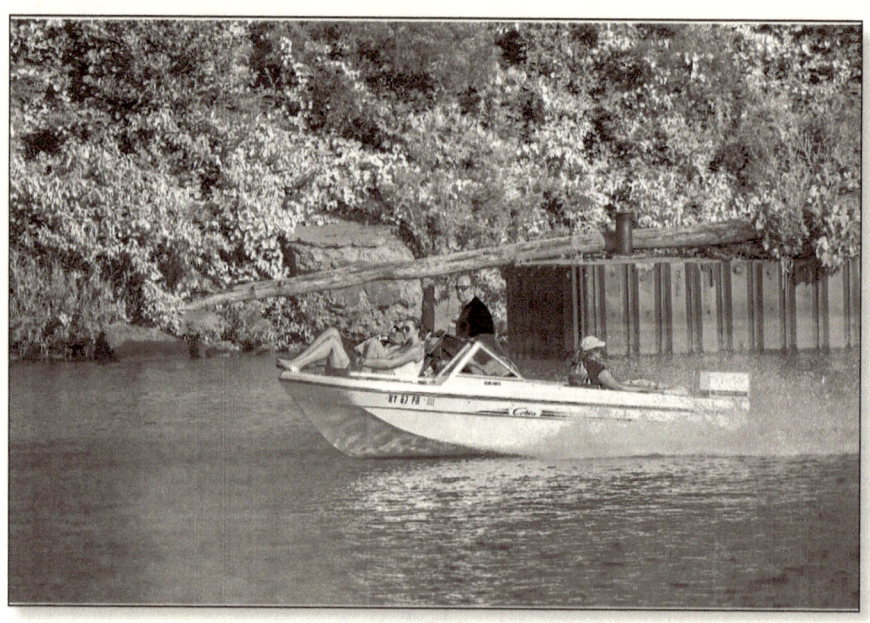

Freeman's Bridge, Schenectady, NY, July 6, 2014
Nikon D1, 300mm (prime), 1/2000, f/4.5, ISO 200, P, center-weighted metering
© 2014, 2015 by Shawn M. Tomlinson

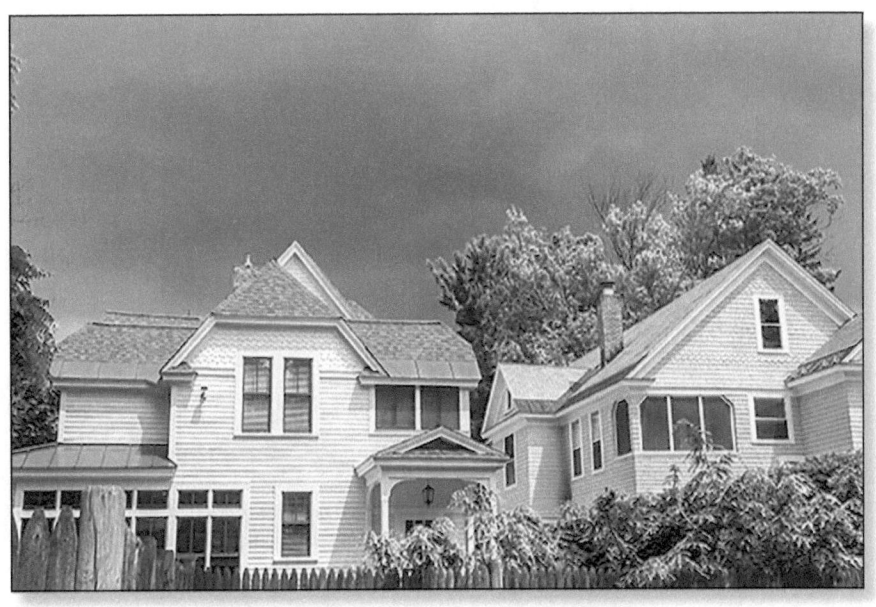

- Bright area washout
- Memory card size limitation (2gb CF card maximum)
- No fill flash (no pro DSLRs have these, even today)
- Batteries hard to find, expensive.
- Charger very expensive and hard to find
- Sensor cleaning requires an AC adapter to lock up the mirror.

The pros far outweigh the cons of the Nikon D1, but that does not diminish the significance of the cons. They will get in your way if you are used to a modern DSLR.

The low resolution, which probably is what keeps most people from wanting or trying a D1 and keeps the price low, really isn't a problem unless you want big printed enlargements.

Keep in mind that, even though the D1's resolution is a little less than 3

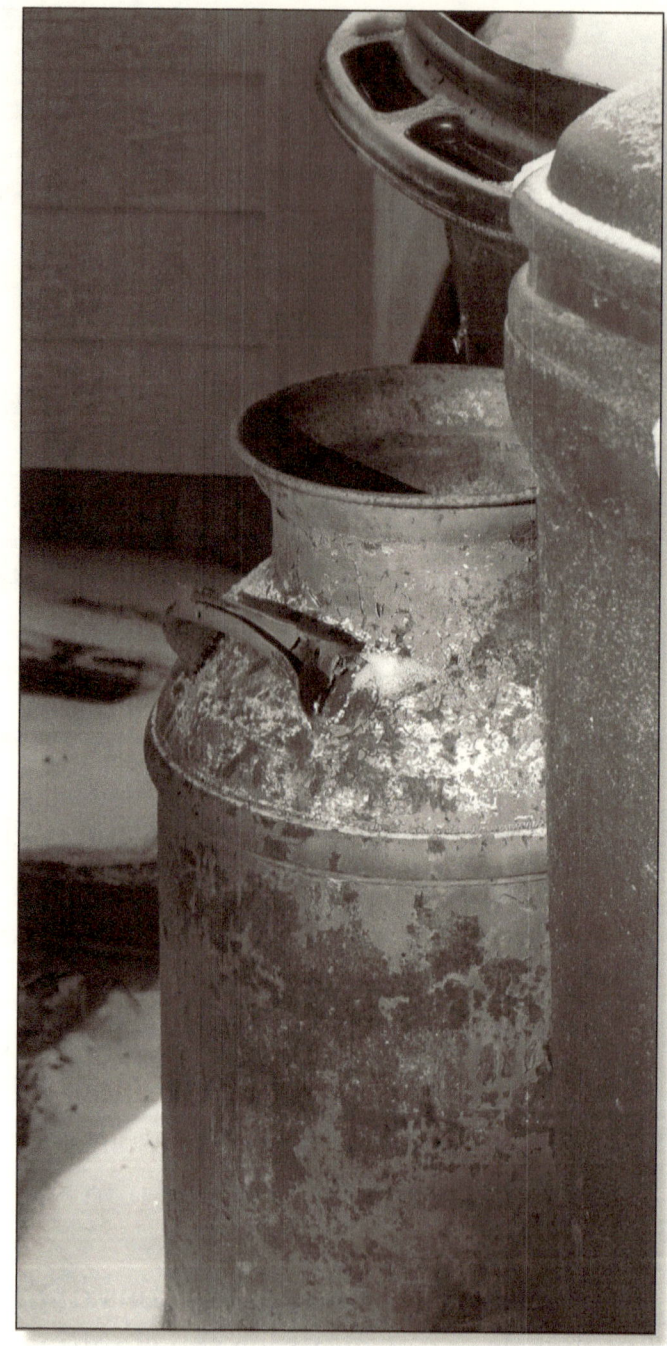

Ballston Lake, NY, May 1, 2014
Nikon D1, 46mm, 1/800, f/5.6, ISO 200, Av, pattern metering
© 2014, 2015 by Shawn M. Tomlinson

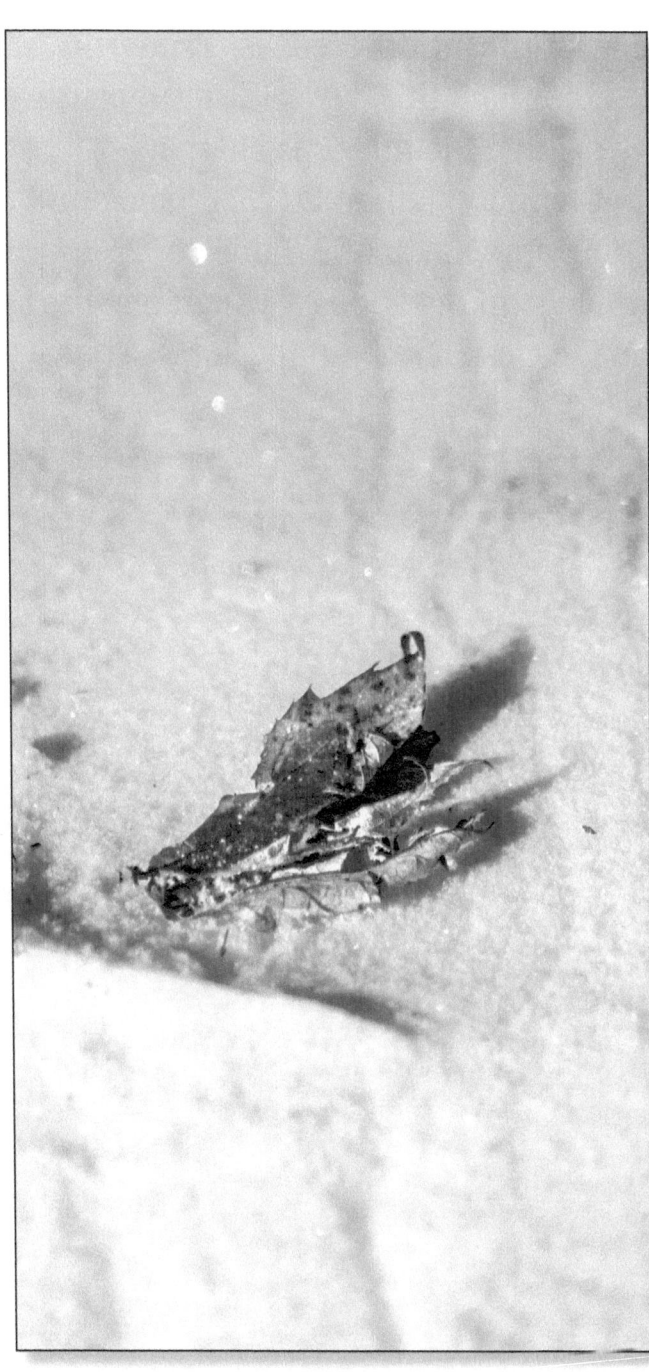

megapixels, its images are far superior to other 3-megapixel cameras because of the professional technology used to build it. In other words, if you compare a RAW image shot with the D1 at full resolution to a JPEG from a point-and-shoot Casio camera, for example, you will notice significant differences. Primarily this means the color is noticeably and significantly better from the D1 and the image is sharper.

When I shoot with the Nikon D1 (2.65 megapixels), D70 (6.1 megapixels) and D7000 (16.2 megapixels), there's no question of which one produces better images, especially in the subtle sharp-

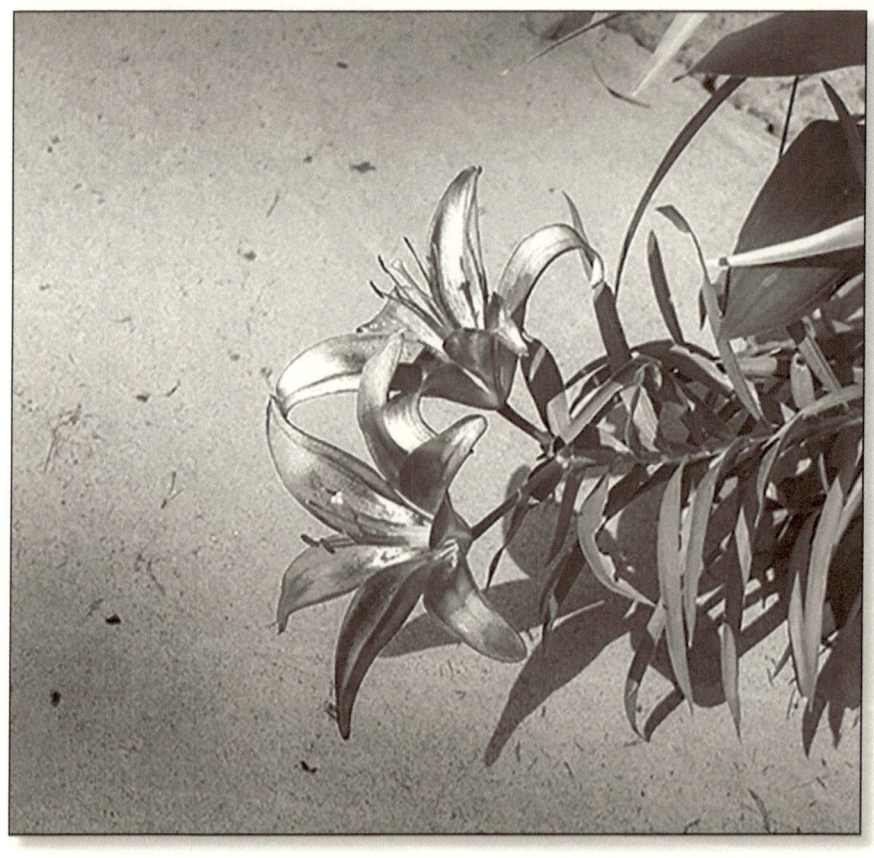

Saratoga Springs, NY, July 1, 2014
Nikon D1, 70mm, 1/640, f/5.3, ISO 200, Av, pattern metering
© 2014, 2015 by Shawn M. Tomlinson

ness in the D7000. However, unless you blow up the images to 100 percent, it is difficult to tell the difference in color, especially between the D1 and D70.

In fact, the lower resolution of the D1 can be an advantage for some subjects. I found, for example, that when I'm shooting macro images of flowers that the slight softness of the D1 — due to fewer megapixels — actually produces brilliant images.

The resolution rarely has gotten in my way.

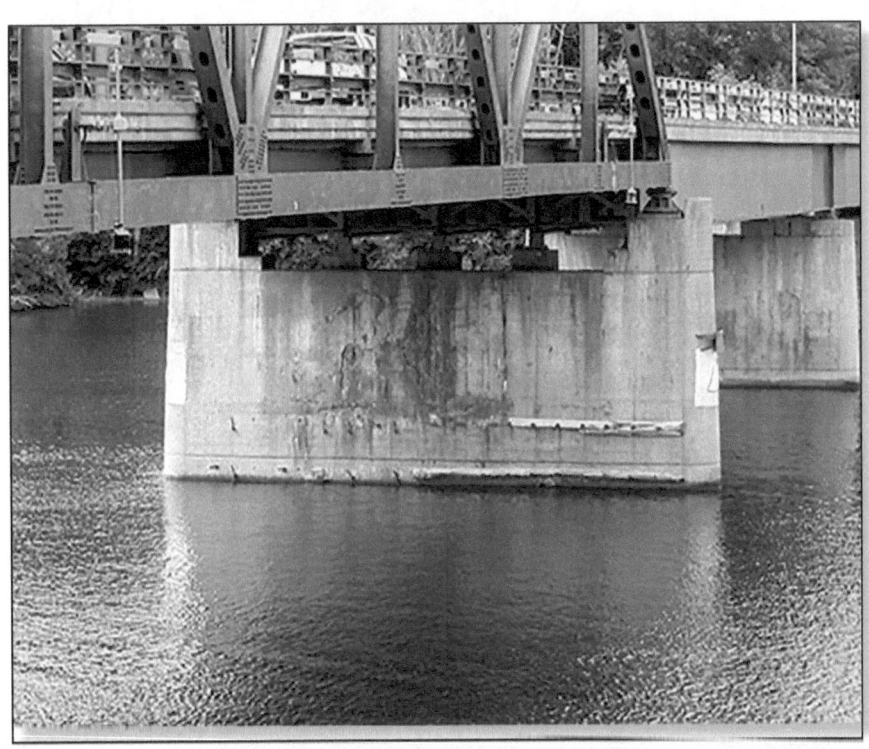

Aqueduct, Rexford, NY, July 16, 2014
Nikon D1, 70mm, 1/160, f/5.3, ISO 200, Av, pattern metering
© 2014, 2015 by Shawn M. Tomlinson

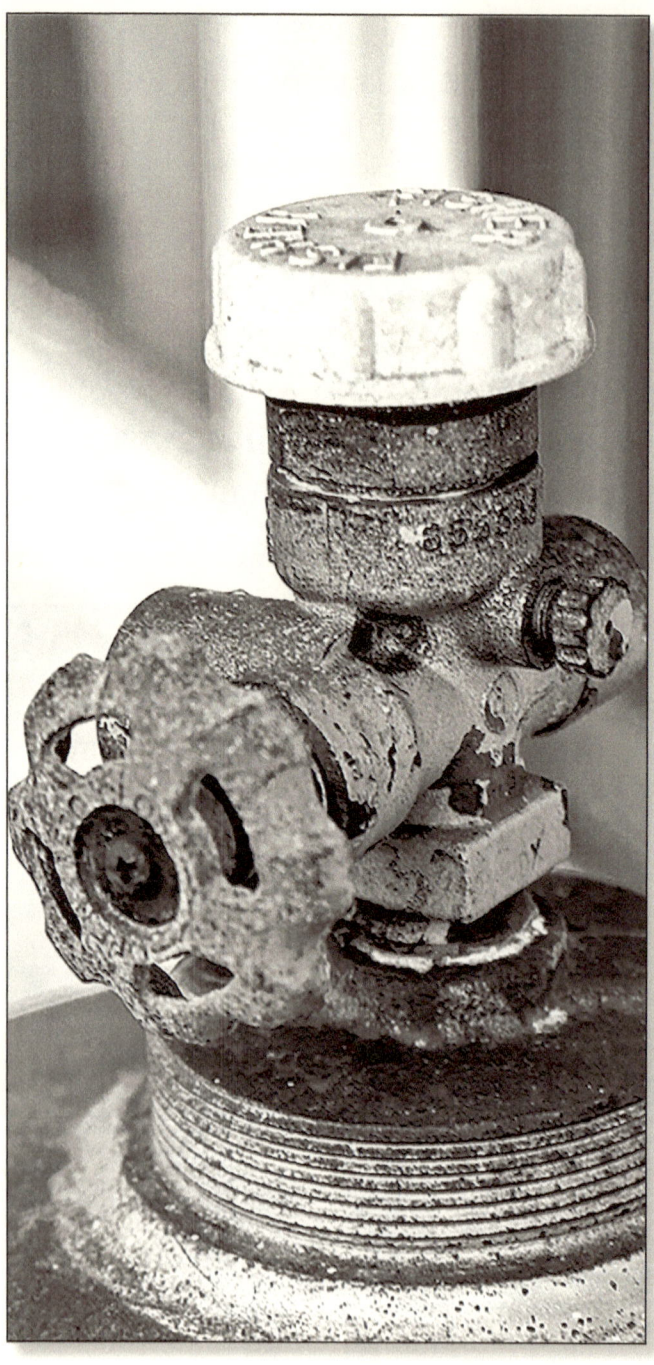

The two things that I do find annoying — but accept as the compromise for being able to afford and use a pro DSLR — are the convoluted menu system and the long buffering time.

The menus on the D1 are annoying because they are all codes. You either have to have the manual

Broadalbin, NY, May 2, 2014
Nikon D1, 82mm, 1/90, f/5.6, ISO 200, Av, pattern metering
© 2014, 2015 by Shawn M. Tomlinson

with you when you shoot or you have to memorize the codes you need. This problem was solved with the upgraded successors to the D1, the D1X and D1H. Still, I really don't need to change many things on the menu, so until I need to, I don't really think about it.

The

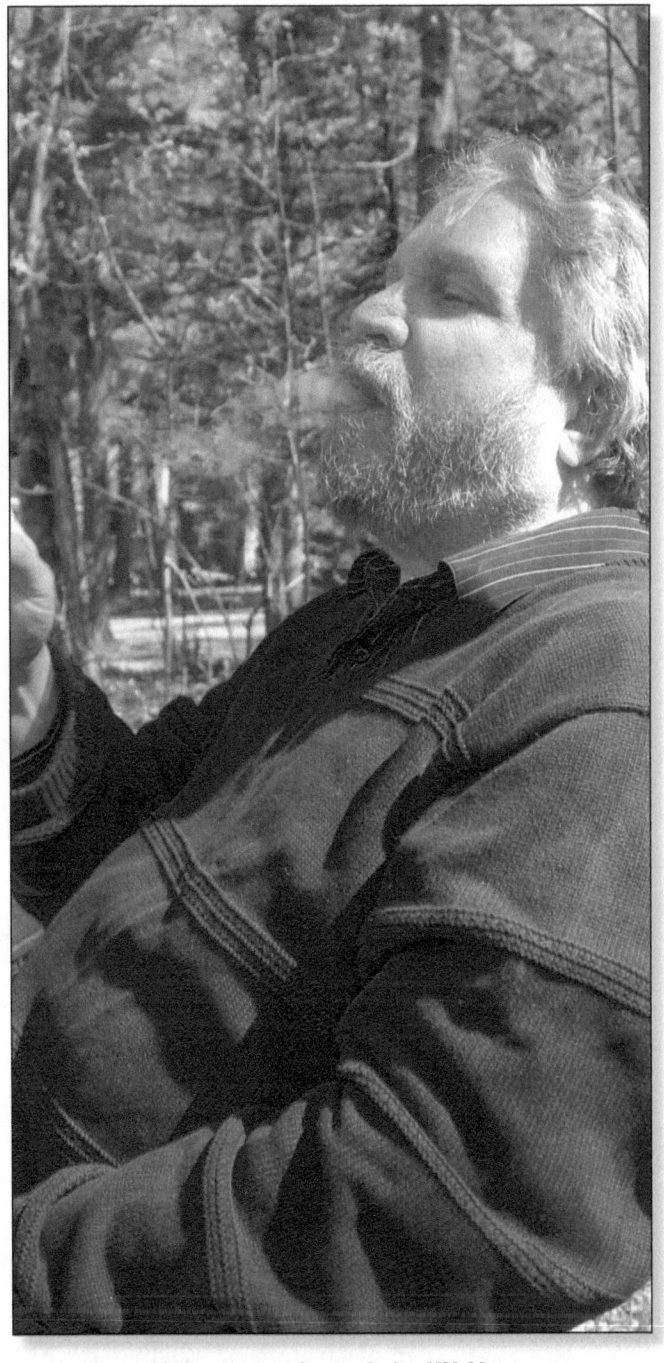

Shawn M. Tomlinson, Caroga Lake, NY, May 20, 2014
Nikon D1, 28mm, 1/320, f/5.6, ISO 400, Av, pattern metering
© 2014, 2015 by Richard H. Nilsen

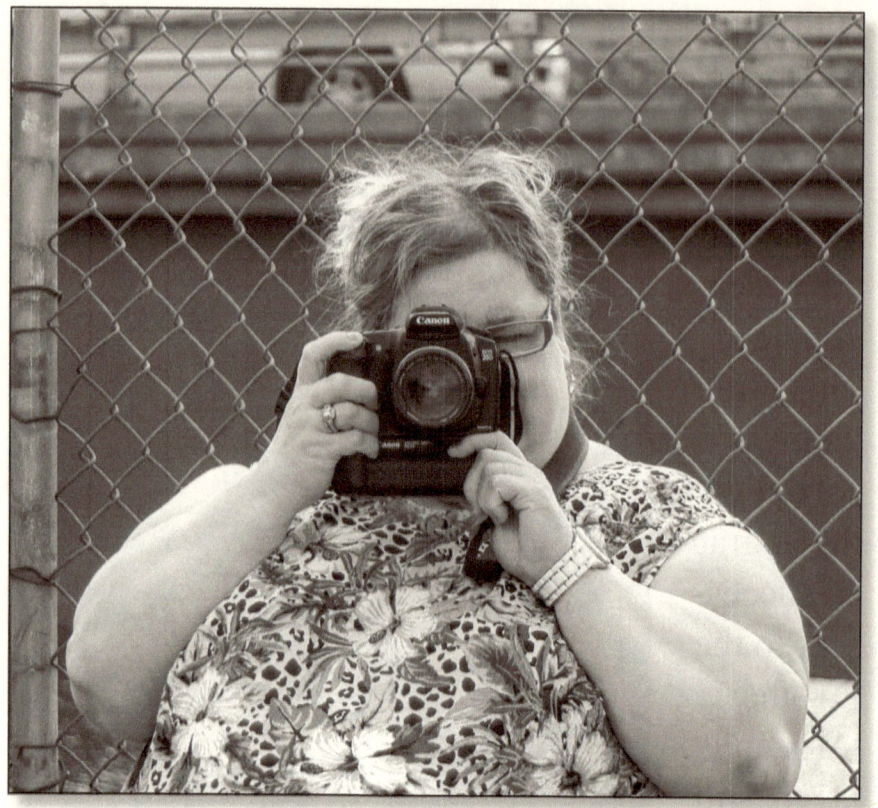

Carole A. Tomlinson, Aqueduct, Rexford, NY, July 16, 2014
Nikon D1, 70mm, 1/350, f/5.3, ISO 200, aperture priority, pattern metering
© 2014, 2015 by Shawn M. Tomlinson

buffering time, however, does get a bit in my way, or, well, did until I figured out a work-around.

What I mean by buffering time is the time it takes after you press the shutter release button until the D1 writes the image to the CF card and the thus the time it takes before you can shoot the next photo. Being as old as it is, and really the first practical DSLR upon which most of today's are based upon, the engineers who designed and built it did not know yet what would and wouldn't get in the way. They also were limited by the technology of the last part of the 20th century.

So, if you shoot with the D1 in "S" or single shot mode, it takes a while for the image to write to the card. While it's doing this, you can't take a photo, so if you like to shoot a lot and fast, you simply can't in the "S" mode.

The way I got around this is by thinking about how I typically shoot. I usually take several images quickly back-to-back, then I don't take any for a few minutes, and then repeat. So, by setting the D1 to "C" or continual mode, the camera works with me. This mode allows me to shoot up to five or six images before it stops to buffer, so I can make my usual shots and when I get to the lull period when I'm not shooting, the D1 uses that time to write the images to the card. Now that I've got the hang of it, this works well.

So, yes, the Nikon D1 is not as easy to use as a Canon EOS Rebel or a Nikon D3300, but, hey, it's a professional DSLR. It wasn't designed to be easy, just to be great.

And it still is.

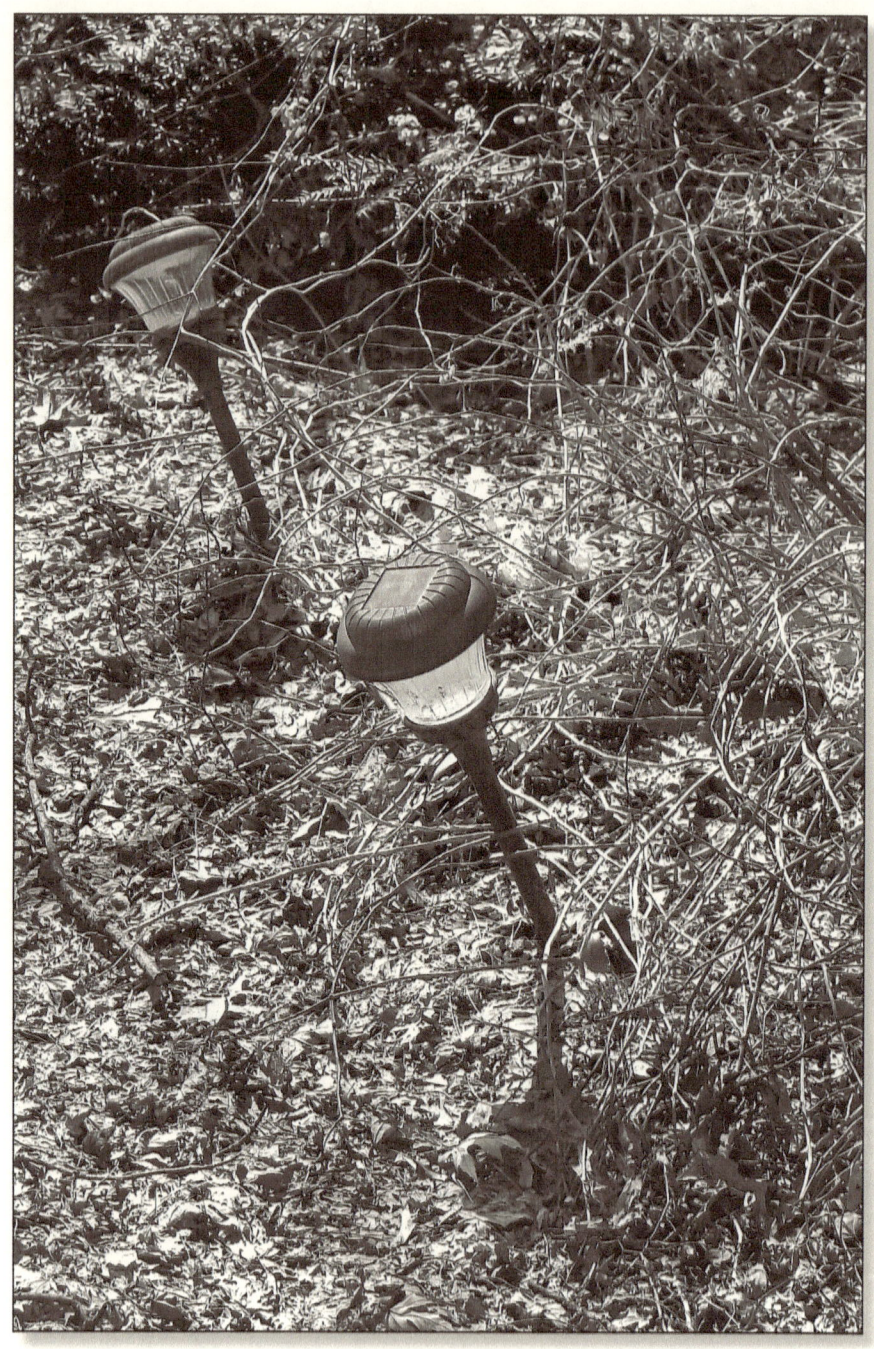

Ballston Lake, NY, April 2, 2014
Nikon D1, 70mm, 1/125, f/11, ISO 200, P, pattern metering
© 2014, 2015 by Shawn M. Tomlinson

Part 3
The Pro Advantage

I was forced into the opportunity recently of revisiting the Nikon D1 because my Nikon D7000 — my main, use-it-every-bloody-day DSLR — died during a shoot. I was devastated and still am.

Because I shoot every day, I couldn't let this get in my way.

I have several other working DSLRs:
- Pentax *ist DS (6.1 megapixels)
- Pentax K20D (14.2 megapixels)
- Canon EOS 20D (8.2 megapixels)
- Nikon D70 (6.1 megapixels)
- Nikon D1 (2.65 megapixels)

Now, from this list, it may appear that the Pentax K20D and its 14.2-megapixel resolution would be the obvious, closest replacement for the 16.2 megapixel Nikon D7000.

The thing is, that isn't what I've been shooting with.

The reason I moved away from Pentax after 32 years with its cameras is that it does not produce the vivid colors that the Nikons do, and it doesn't focus nearly as quickly, especially in non-ideal lighting conditions.

The Nikon D1 focuses fast. Very fast. It's a *pro* DSLR.

So, I took my favorite lens, a prime Nikon AF D 28mm f/2.8, and got out there shooting.

I'd never used a prime lens on it before and the

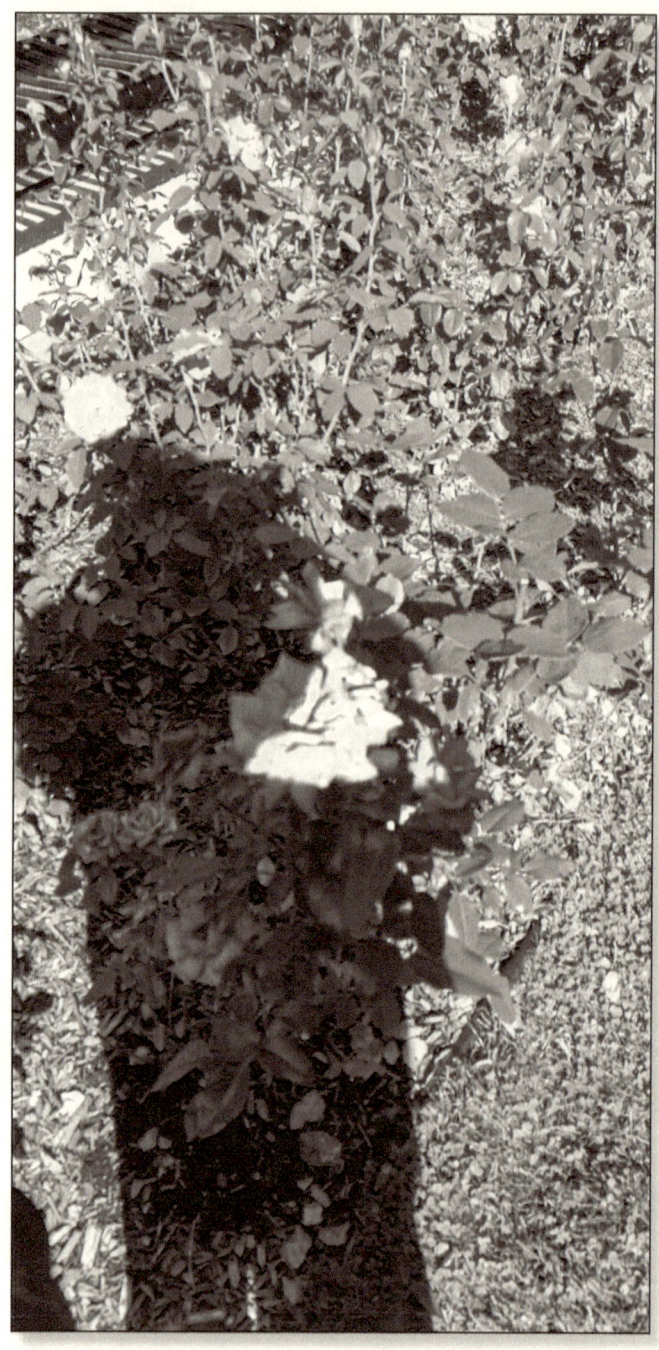

Rose Garden, Central Park, Schenectady, NY, Aug. 17, 2014
Nikon D1, 18mm, 1/400, f/5.6, ISO 200, Av, pattern metering
© 2014, 2015 by Shawn M. Tomlinson

sharpness improvement really showed. It almost always does, no matter what DSLR you use, with a prime lens. This lens makes my entry-level D70 sharper, too.

I hadn't shot with the D1 in a while, not since I had been using the D7000.

It was like shooting with a new camera.

Holding the D1 in my hands was and always is a joy. I like the tough build and weight of it. I like the resounding sound it makes when I press the shutter release.

And the images?

Yes, OK, 2.65-megapixel resolution is not quite

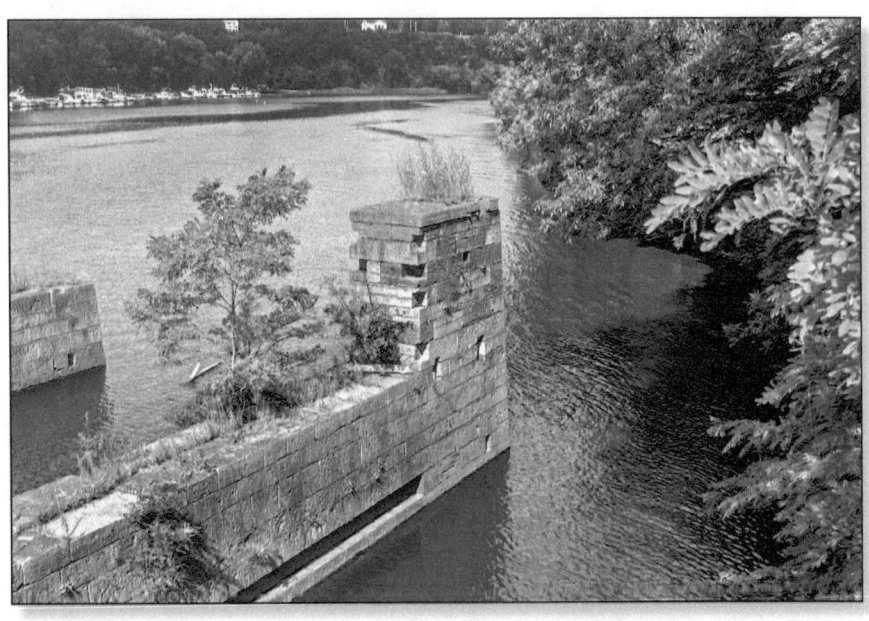

Aqueduct, Rexford, NY, July 16, 2014
Nikon D1, 28mm, 1/1250, f/3.5, ISO 200, Av, pattern metering
© 2014, 2015 by Shawn M. Tomlinson

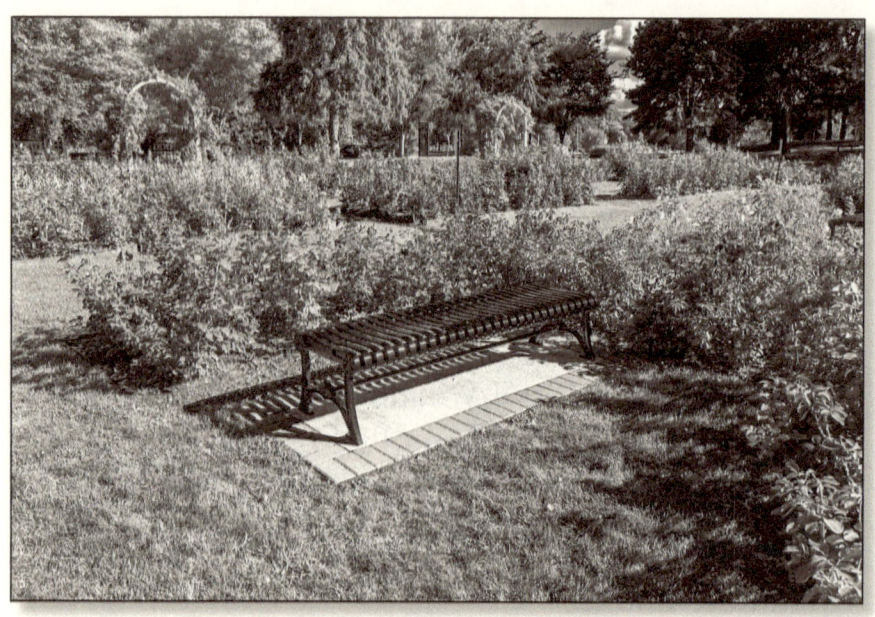

Rose Garden, Central Park, Schenectady, NY, Aug. 17, 2014
Nikon D1, 18mm, 1/500, f/5.6, ISO 200, Av, pattern metering
© 2014, 2015 by Shawn M. Tomlinson

as sharp as 16.2, but the images are very good, especially the color.

The key, of course, as I reiterate in everything I write about digital photography, is following the two **ABSOLUTE RULES** for serious shooting:

1) **ALWAYS** shoot in **RAW**.

2) **ALWAYS** shoot at the **LOWEST POSSIBLE ISO** sensitivity setting.

It isn't the easiest thing to figure out how to set the D1 to RAW — it takes two separate actions to do it in the esoteric menus — but it is worth the headache.

When I first had the D1, I could not figure out —

even with the manual — how to set it to RAW. So, I was shooting in TIFF and the colors were lifeless and drab. I had to punch them up a lot in Adobe Photoshop to get them close to reality.

The reason images in TIFF or JPEG in DSLRs have dull colors is because the cameras determine a

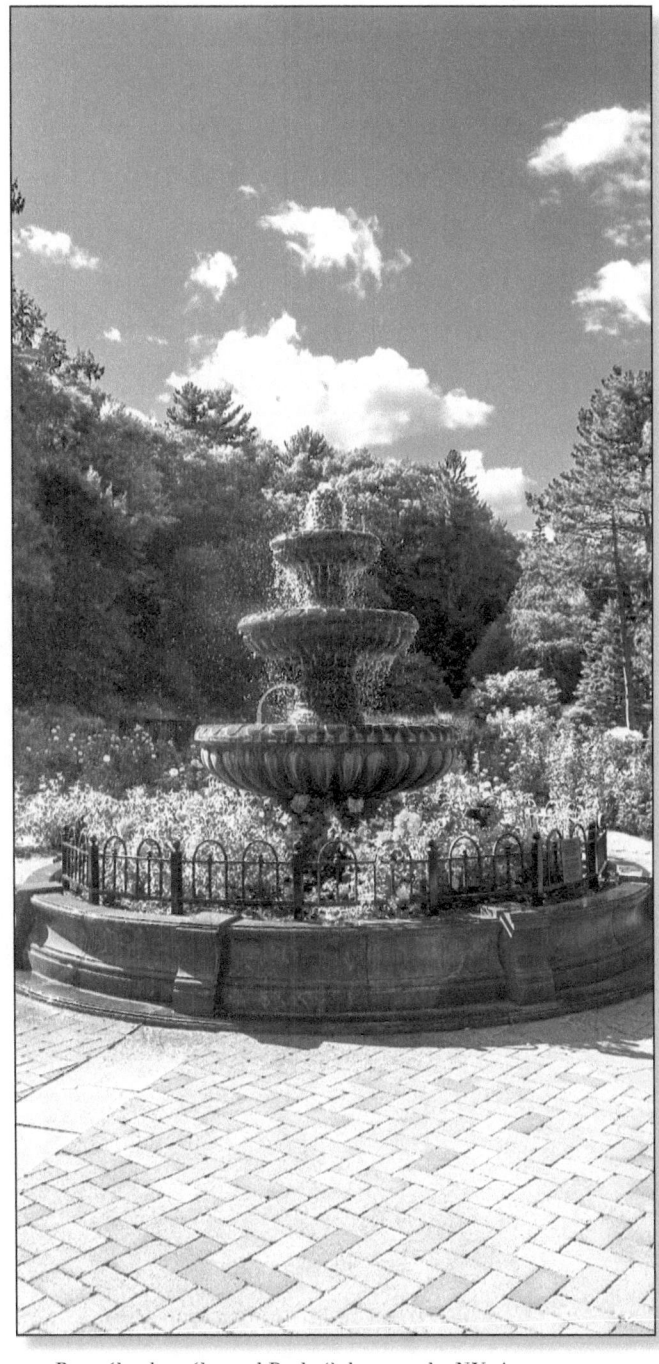

Rose Garden, Central Park, Schenectady, NY, Aug. 17, 2014
Nikon D1, 18mm, 1/500, f/5.6, ISO 200, Av, pattern metering
© 2014, 2015 by Shawn M. Tomlinson

balance of what you set and produce a compromise image. When you capture your images in RAW format, all the data is recorded, which gives you much greater latitude in fine-tuning them. The color straight from the camera in RAW always is better than in JPEG or TIFF.

This is more difficult than it needs to be, but still doable. Here's how to set the D1 to record RAW images:

1) Press the "CSM" (custom function) button on the rear panel at the bottom of the camera.

2) While pressing the "CSM" button, turn the

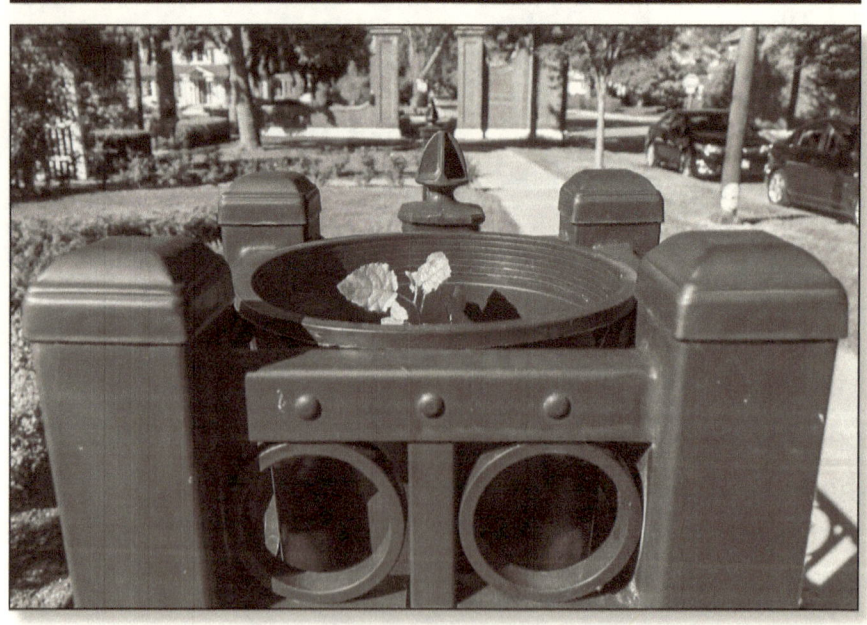

Rose Garden, Central Park, Schenectady, NY, Aug. 17, 2014
Nikon D1, 18mm, 1/500, f/5.6, ISO 200, Av, pattern metering
© 2014, 2015 by Shawn M. Tomlinson

rear Command dial to select custom function "28" shown on the rear small LCD near the bottom next to the buttons.

3) Use the front Sub-Command dial to change it from "0" to "1."

No, you're not done.

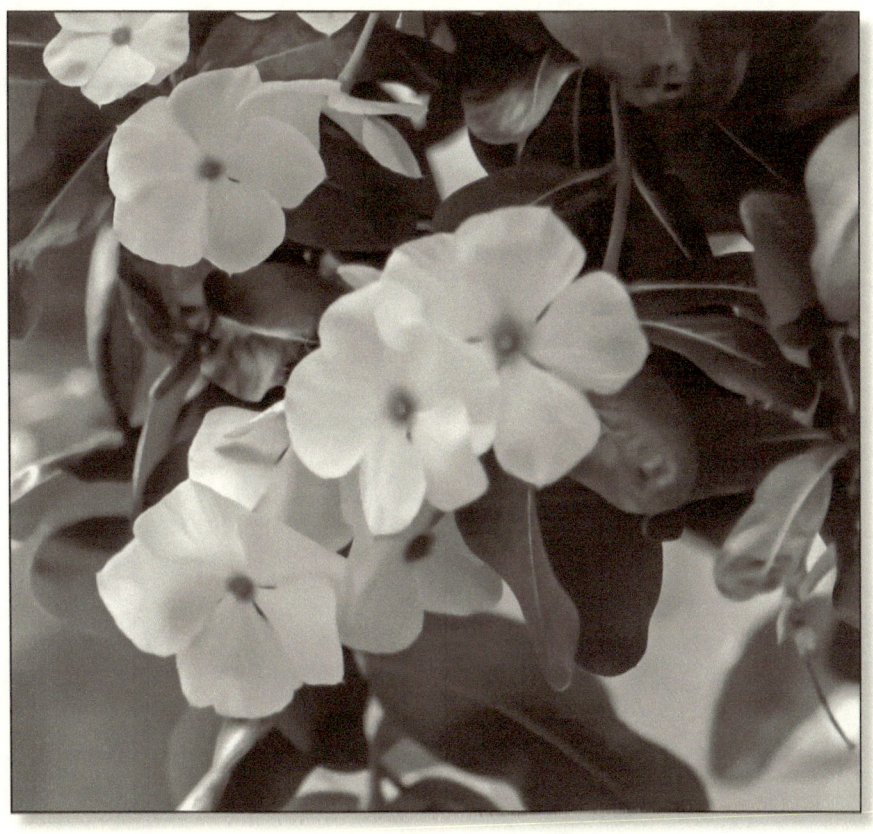

Saratoga Springs, NY, Aug. 5, 2014
Nikon D1, 300mm, 1/1250, f/5.6, ISO 200, S, pattern metering
© 2014, 2015 by Shawn M. Tomlinson

4) Press the "QUAL" (quality) button on that same panel at the lower back.

5) While holding it, turn the Command dial (rear) until the small LCD at the back posts the cryptic "2.7r" message.

Not exactly intuitive.

Still, as I said, it is worth it because once you start shooting in RAW, you will be astonished at the color you will get from the ancient Nikon D1.

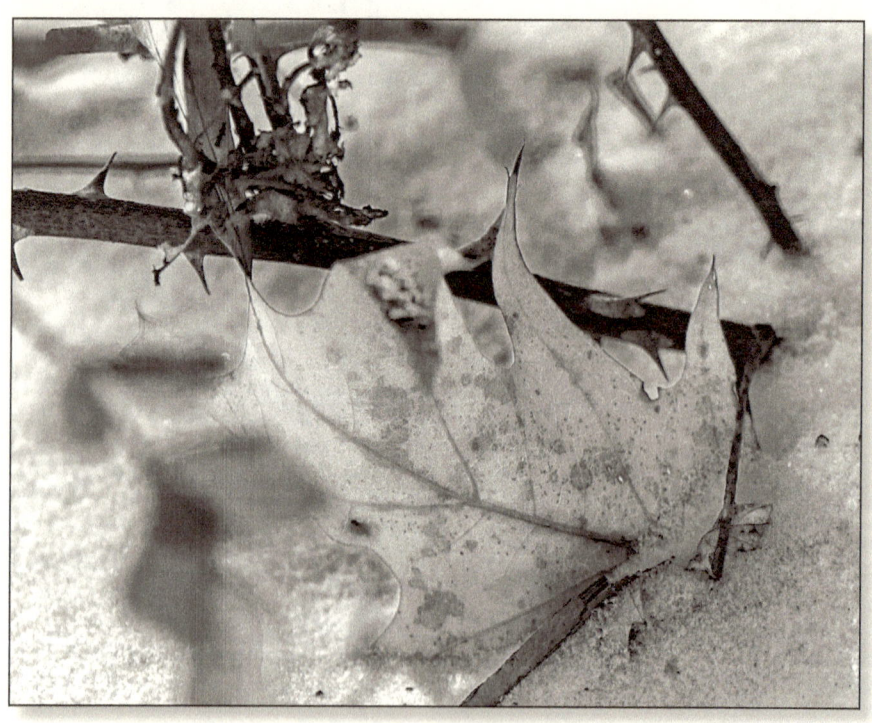

Ballston Lake, NY, Jan. 8, 2015
Nikon D1, 270mm, 1/320, f/5.3, ISO 800, M, pattern metering
© 2015 by Shawn M. Tomlinson

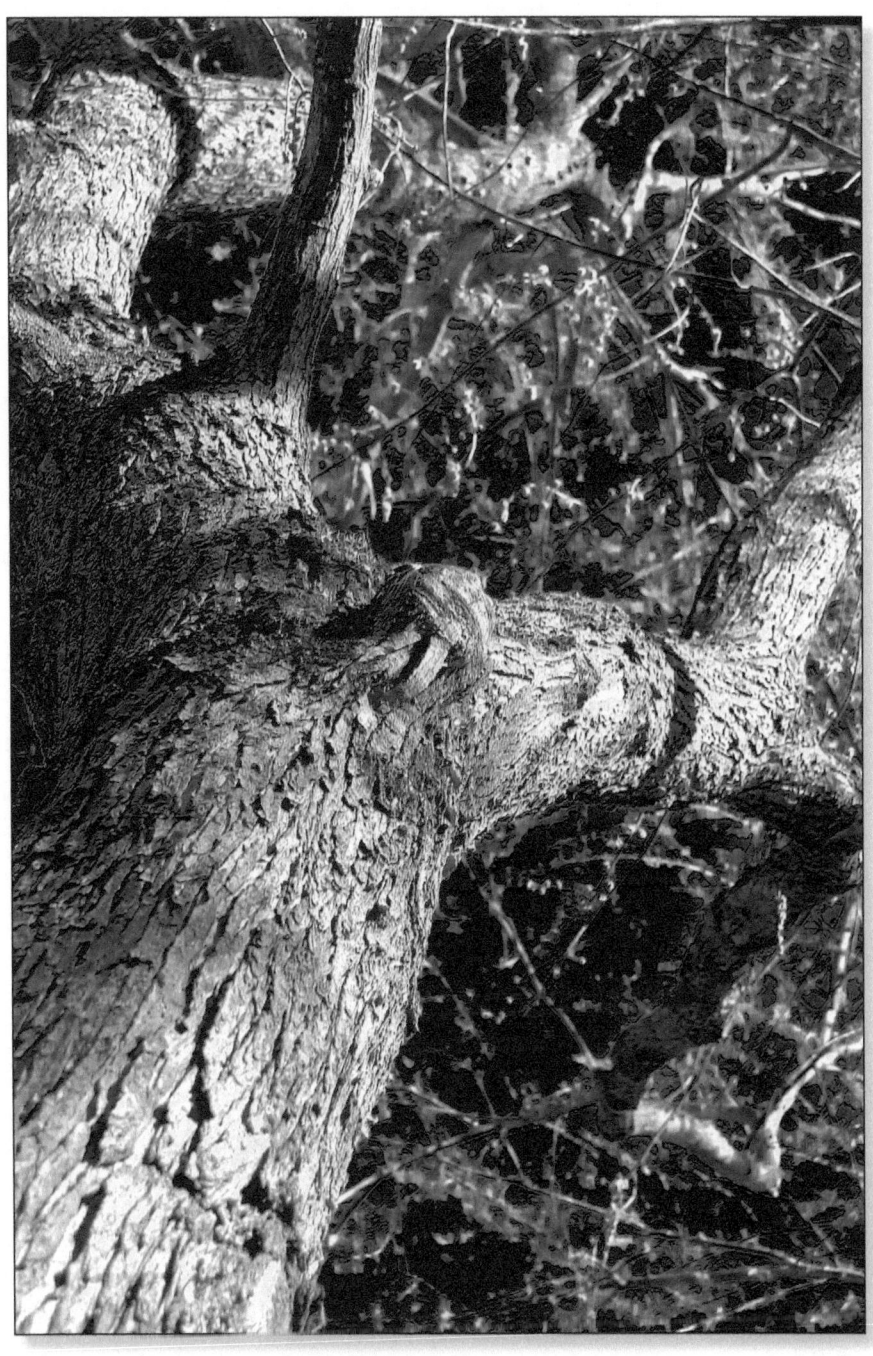

Ballston Lake, NY, April 2, 2014
Nikon D1, 70mm, 1/180, f/6.7, ISO 200, P, pattern metering
© 2014, 2015 by Shawn M. Tomlinson

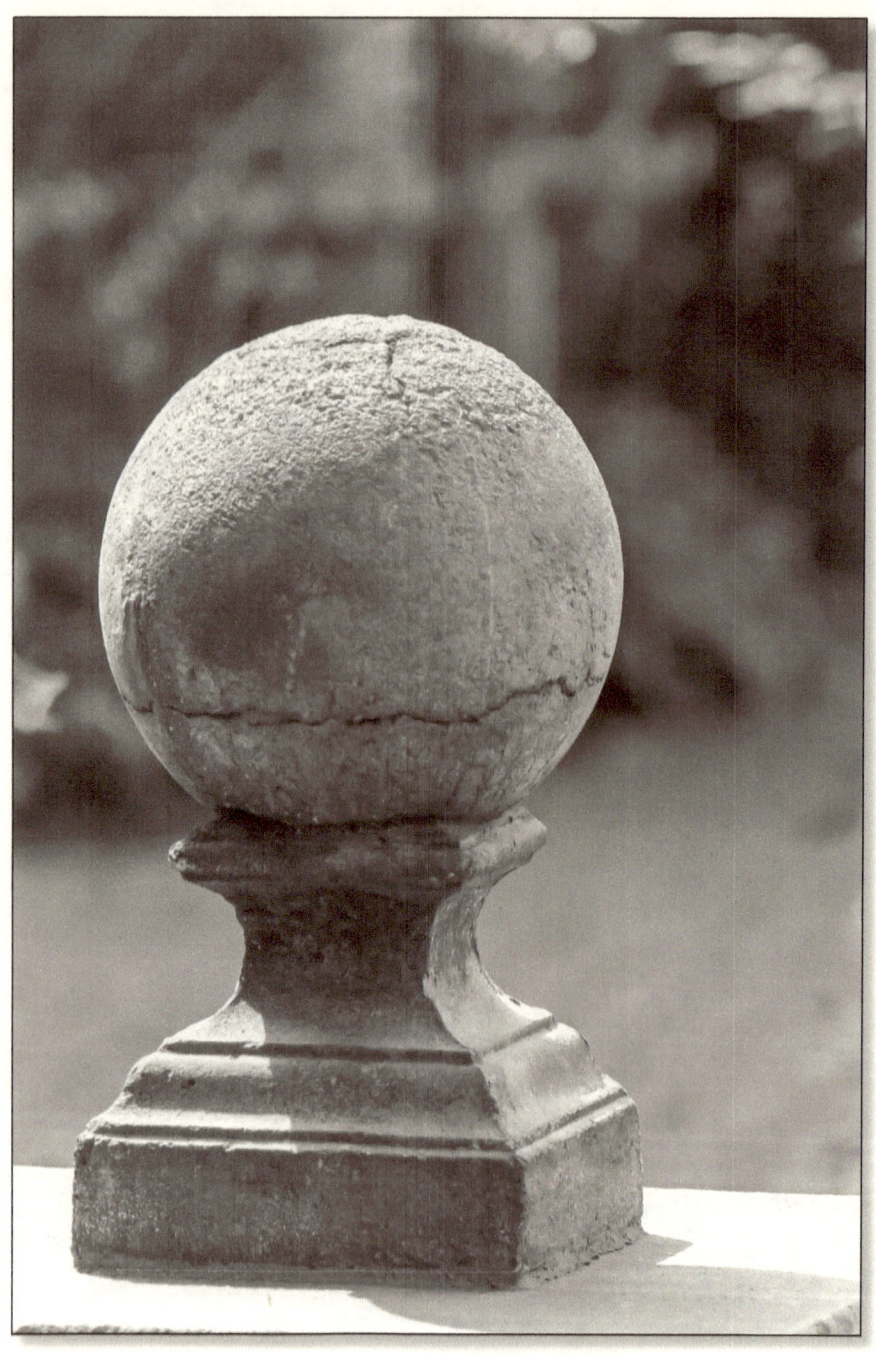

Saratoga Springs, NY, Aug. 5, 2014
Nikon D1, 180mm, 1/1250, f/4.8, ISO 200, S, pattern metering
© 2014, 2015 by Shawn M. Tomlinson

Part 4
The Last Details

So, OK, you're ready to turn pro with the Nikon D1.

There are a few details to consider before jumping onto eBay.

1) The Nikon D1 is old. If you get a good one, you will not be disappointed. But it's old, so some of them have quit working or have problems.

Mine, for example, has a problem on the sensor with a white line over to the left side of the images where pixels are dead or "hot." This annoys me, but never stops me using the camera. Unless the left side of the image is dark, it isn't visible, and if it is, it's close enough to the left edge to just crop it out.

This is the only problem I have with the camera, but it is annoying.

You are buying a used DSLR from the last century, so if you buy on eBay, you're taking a risk.

If you buy from a reputable dealer such as KEH. com, you can rest assured the seller has tested and graded appropriately the camera. And, if there is a problem with it they did not discover, they will replace or repair it, or refund your money. Yes, this will cost a bit more than eBay, but from my own experience, it is worth it.

I knew about KEH and had bought equipment from the company previously, but I was stupid and bid upon a D1 on eBay. I got it cheap, too: $57!

However, it turned out to have the sensor pixel problem, and the real problem, which is it did not come with a charger. Again, I was stupid. I assumed it did have a charger because usually eBayers say when a DSLR doesn't have one.

Besides, I thought, how much could a charger

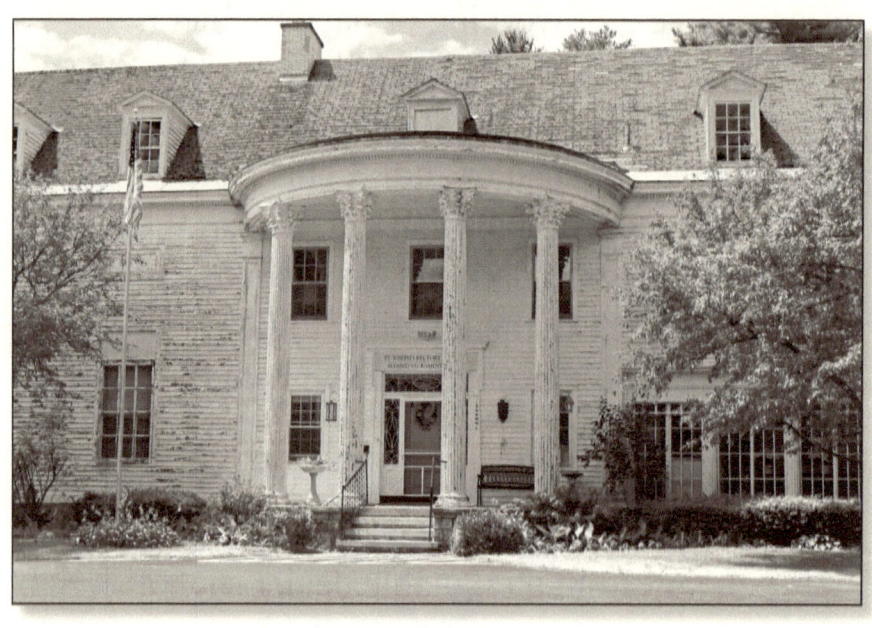

Broadalbin House, Broadalbin, NY, July 18, 2014
Nikon D1, 34mm, 1/1250, f/3.8, ISO 200, Av, pattern metering
© 2014, 2015 by Shawn M. Tomlinson

be?

The answer: A lot.

2) The battery and charger thing, along with a warranty, are the things to consider when buying a D1. That's why my cautionary tale should tell you that you need to buy from a dealer, not an eBay seller.

KEH — the best photographic equipment dealer — generally supplies a battery and charger with used cameras. For this, of course, they charge a bit more. When the company doesn't supply these things, it states it clearly and discounts the price.

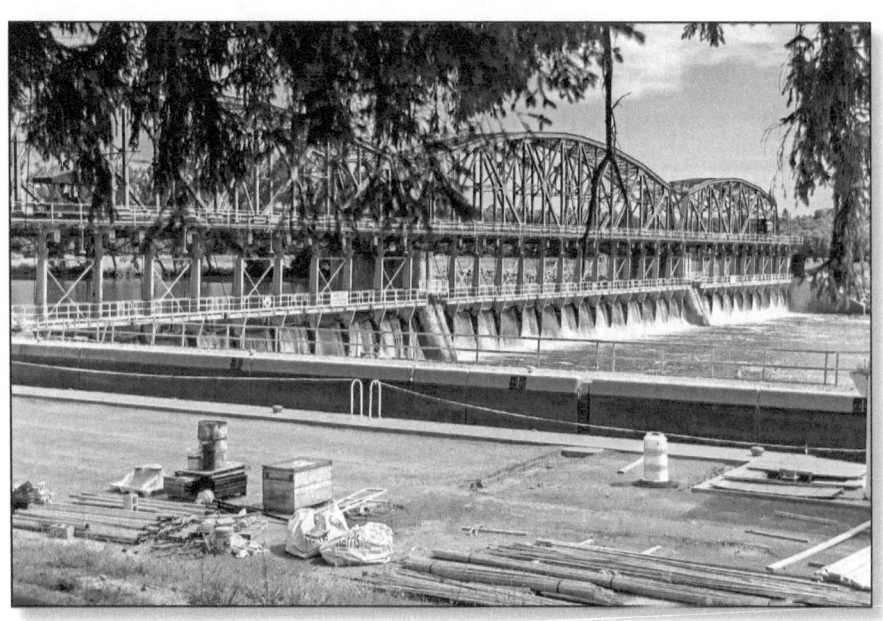

Lock 8, Rotterdam, NY, July 20, 2014
Nikon D1, 31mm, 1/1600, f/3.5, ISO 200, Av, pattern metering
© 2014, 2015 by Shawn M. Tomlinson

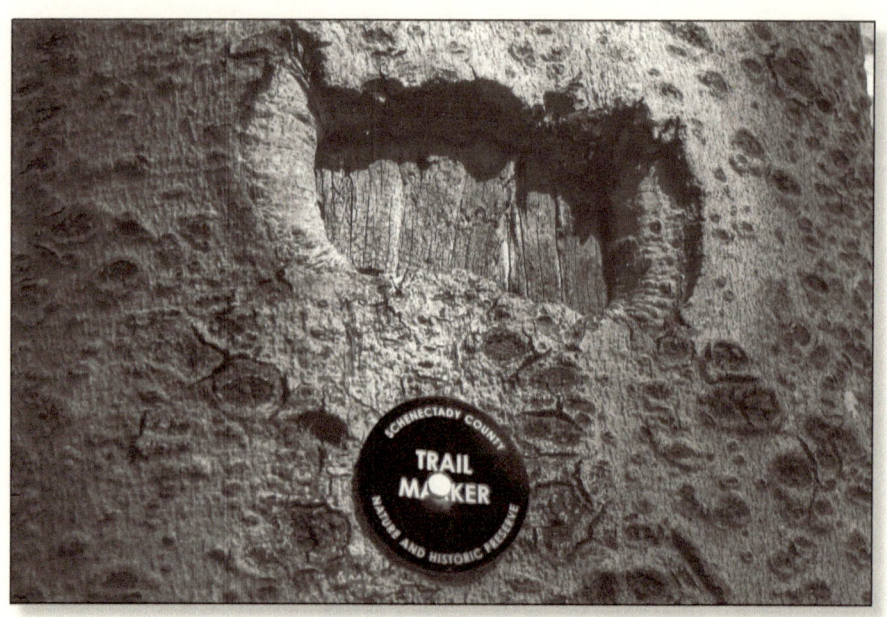

Indian Kill Nature Preserve, Glenville, NY, July 21, 2014
Nikon D1, 60mm, 1/90, f/5, ISO 200, Av, pattern metering
© 2014, 2015 by Shawn M. Tomlinson

Typically, KEH charged about $110 for a Nikon D1 with a used but working battery and the charger.

Sounds like a lot more than my $57 deal, right?

The charger alone, when you can find one, usually costs about $100. The battery, again when you can find one, usually costs at least $30. So, suddenly my $57 deal costs $187, $77 more than if I bought the D1 from KEH.

I didn't do it quite that way. I bid — again stupidly — on a Nikon D1H with five batteries and a charger that I won for $125 plus $25 shipping. Which would have solved all my problems with the D1 and given me one of its successors, the D1H, to

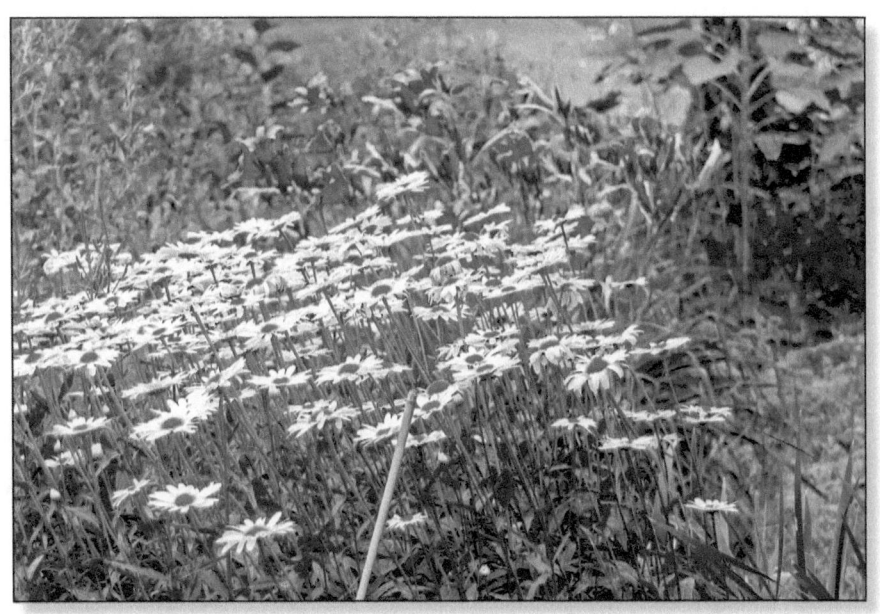

use.

It did solve the charger problem and gave me some more batteries — none of which last very long — but the D1H did not work. Well, it works fine as a camera, but just will not write to or read a memory card. The only fix for that, apparently, is getting a different D1H, and that's not worth it.

Anyway, my $57 deal cost $207 in the end. Much more than I should have or would have paid.

So, if you are going to look on eBay for a D1, make sure it comes with a working battery and charger. Or be smarter than me and buy from KEH or another actual store, be it online or real.

3) SecureDigital (SD) memory cards pretty much have become the standard in cameras, smartphones and other devices. They didn't even exist when the D1 was made, so it takes the older, better CompactFlash (CF) memory cards. You can't find those in big box stores anymore, only

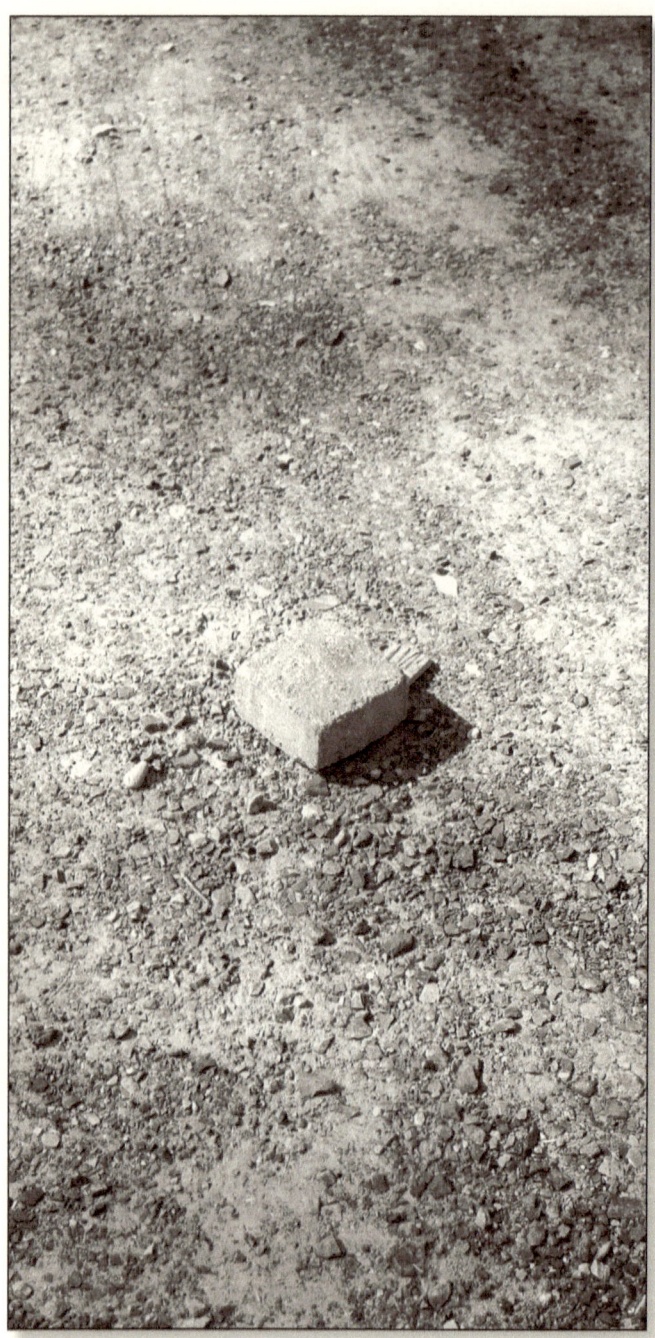

Indian Kill Nature Preserve, Glenville, NY, July 21, 2014
Nikon D1, 38mm, 1/1250, f/4, ISO 200, Av, pattern metering
© 2014, 2015 by Shawn M. Tomlinson

usually on-line, or per-haps, if you are lucky enough to have an actual, physical camera store near you, there.

But wait, there's less!

CF cards still were new in 1999 when the D1 came out. They didn't have the kind of capacity they do now. They had 64mb or 128mb capacities.

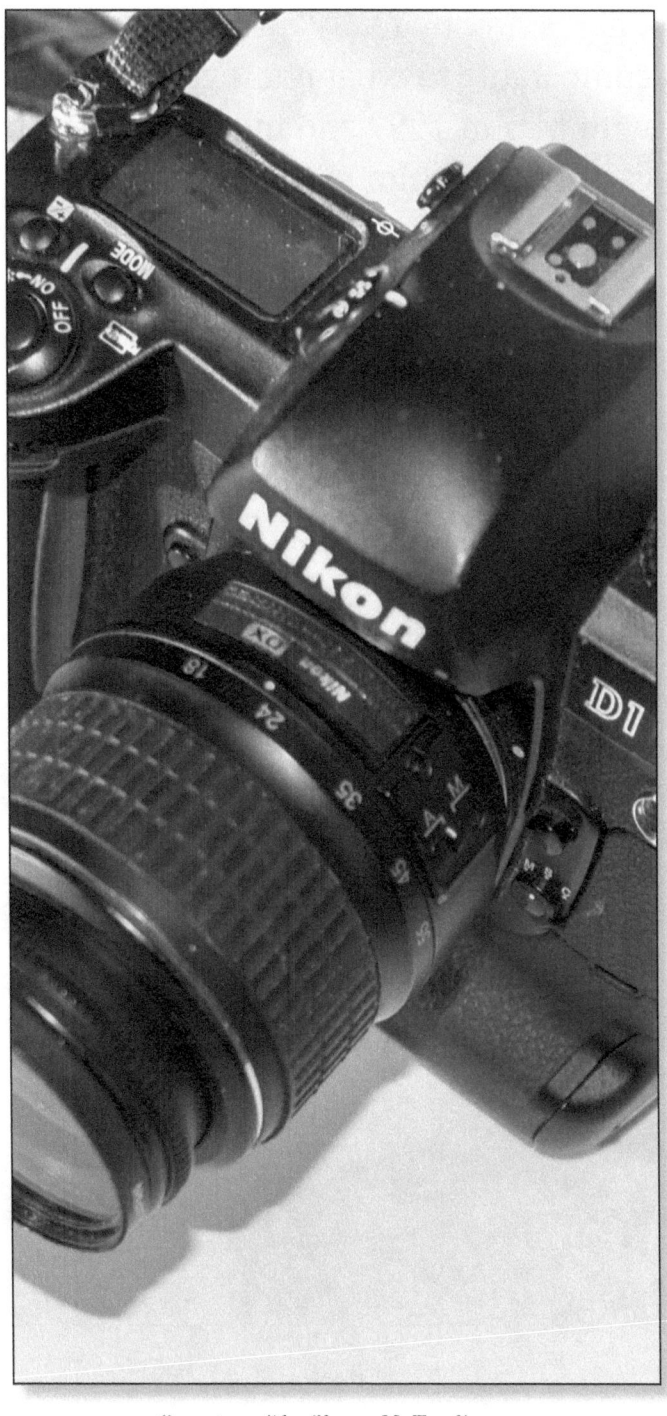

That is tiny by today's standards, but they were comparable to what photographers were getting with film in 1999 and the D1 was the transition camera from film to digital.

Yes, you can use larger capacity CF cards than those with the D1, but not by much. The maximum CF capacity card for the D1 is 2gb. If you put a 4gb or larger card in, the D1 either won't read it at all or will use 2gb and not the rest. It will tell you the card is full when you know it is not, but there's no reasoning with it. It knows best.

Still, RAW images at 2.65 megapixels are only about 4mb, so you get quite a few on a 2gb card.

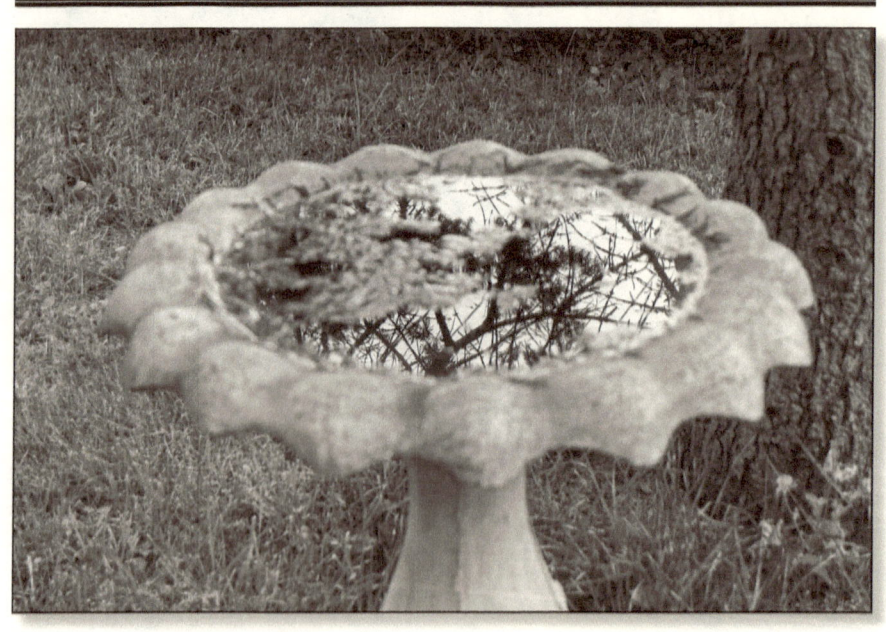

Ballston Lake, NY, July 29, 2014
Nikon D1, 50mm, 1/125, f/5.6, ISO 400, Av, pattern metering
© 2014, 2015 by Shawn M. Tomlinson

I get about 249. Obviously, shooting in JPEG will get you more, but why have a pro DSLR and shoot in JPEG? That's like driving your Ferrari only back and forth to drop the kids off at school.

You can use virtually any capacity CF card up to 2gb, and 2gb CF cards still are reasonably cheap. You can find them online at places such as Amazon and eBay, as well as at camera dealer websites.

Note that CF cards have one Achilles heel, which is that they have many tiny holes that accept the pins in the camera and the card reader. It is relatively easy to bend these pins, especially in card readers, if you aren't careful.

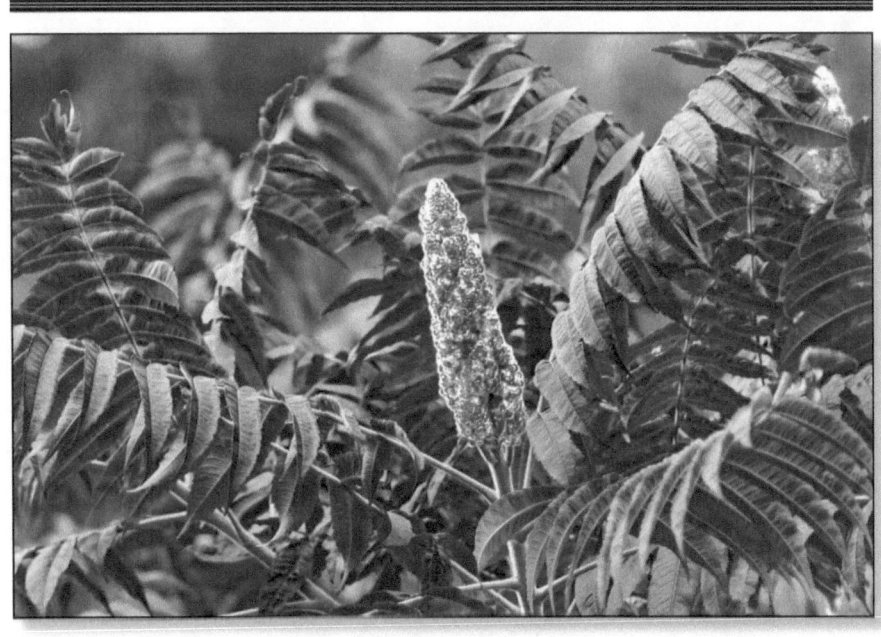

Ballston Lake, NY, July 30, 2014
Nikon D1, 270mm, 1/200, f/5.3, ISO 200, Av, pattern metering
© 2014, 2015 by Shawn M. Tomlinson

4)

The lens. Chances are you will not get a lens with your Nikon D1, unless you spend more for a pack-age deal on eBay. If you al-ready have a Nikon DSLR, your lenses from that will work on the D1.

If you have lens-es for an old Nikon film SLR, chances are those

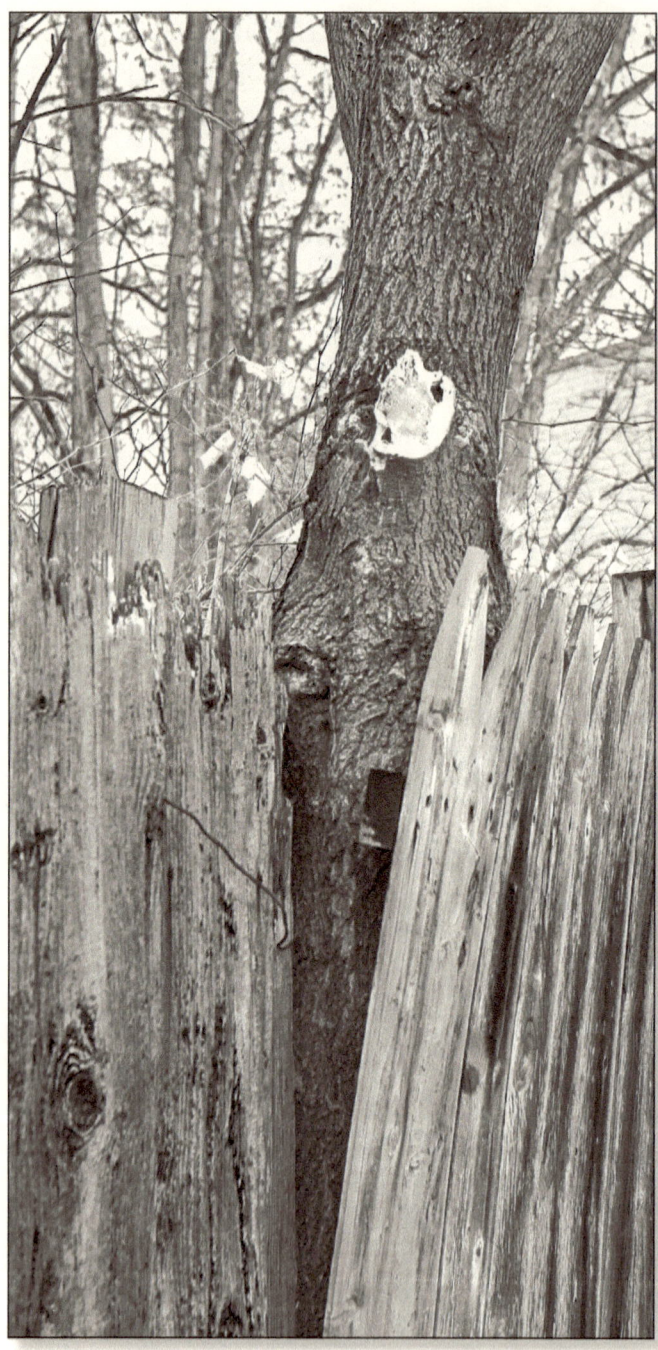

Saratoga Springs, NY, Dec. 13, 2014
Nikon D1, 28mm (prime), 1/160, f/5.6, ISO 200, Av, pattern metering
© 2014, 2015 by Shawn M. Tomlinson

lenses will work as well. The only lenses that do not work that Nikon made are the "invasive" fish-eye lenses — the back of the lens sticks into the camera body and would break the mirror — and what are termed non-AI Nikon lenses. These are the early lenses built from 1959 to

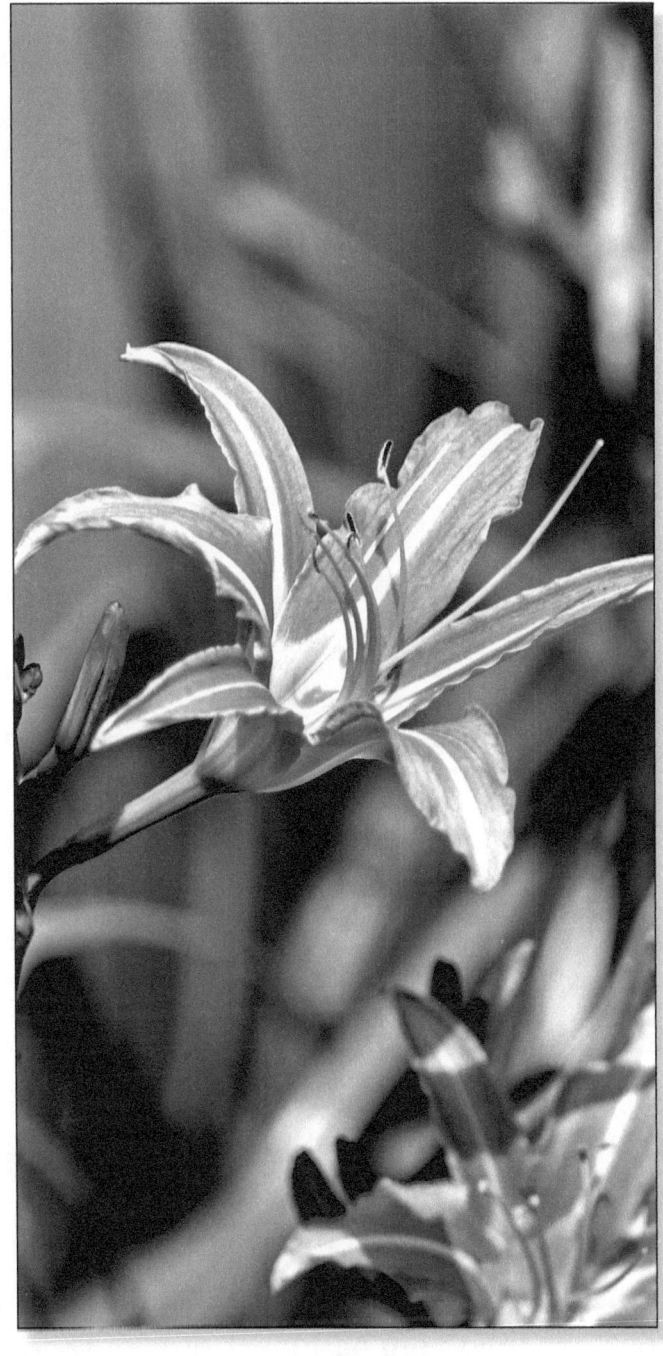

Ballston Lake, NY, July 30, 2014
Nikon D1, 300mm, 1/800, f/5.6, ISO 200, Av, pattern metering
© 2014, 2015 by Shawn M. Tomlinson

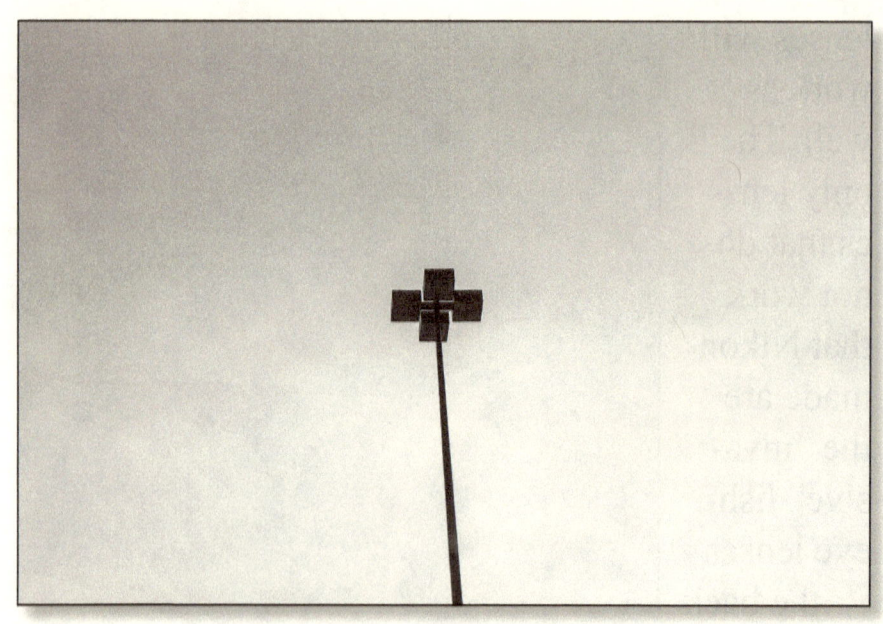

the early 1970s. They have strange-looking prong acceptors on the aperture ring and only one set of aperture numbers. The metal acceptor thingy coupled with a prong sticking out of Nikon, Nikkormat and Nikomat cameras allowed the camera to adjust its meter according to which lens was being used.

Nikon kept the prong-acceptor concept for a while, but started making auto-indexing (AI) lenses. You can tell the difference between non-AI and AI lenses because close to the lens mount, the AI lenses have a second, identical set of aperture numbers and the non-AI lenses don't. As long as that second set of aperture numbers is there, the lens

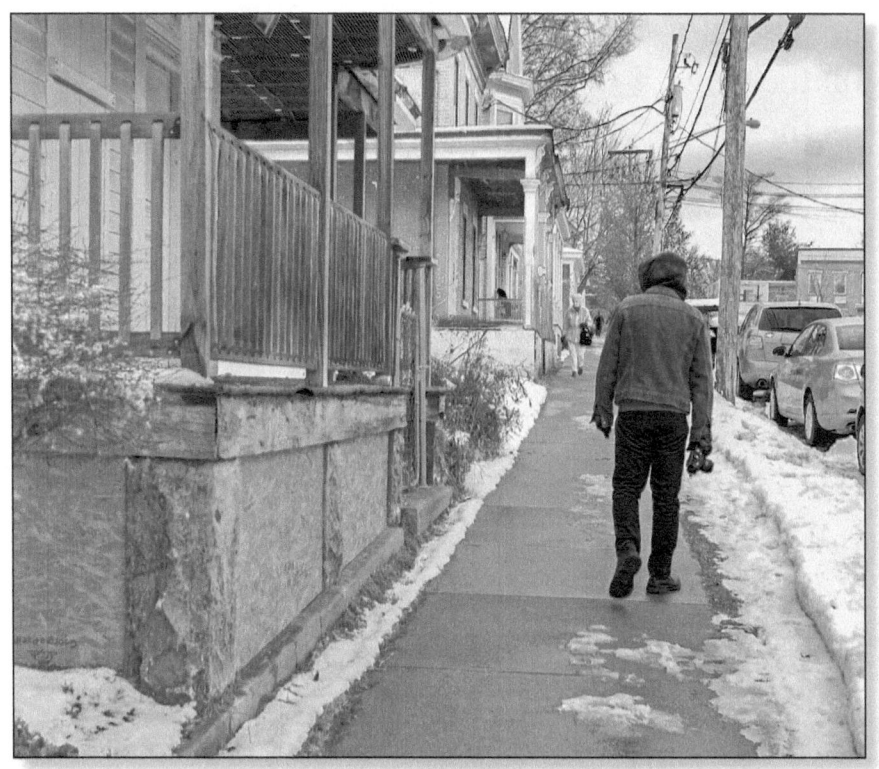

Gary W. Ziroli, Saratoga Springs, NY, Dec. 13, 2014
Nikon D1, 28mm, 1/160, f/5.6, ISO 200, Av, pattern metering
© 2014, 2015 by Shawn M. Tomlinson

will work on the D1.

And, naturally, any Nikon lens without the odd apparatus as long as it is for the "F" mount, also will work, such as Series E and later lenses. Oh, not lenses labeled Pronea, though. This was an oddball camera from Nikon and the lenses work on nothing except Pronea.

You will have to focus manual lenses manually, of course, and it is best to use aperture-priority (A) mode on the D1. This allows you to manually set the aperture on the ring on the lens and the camera sets the shutter speed accordingly. You also can go to full manual (M) mode on the D1 and set the aperture and shutter speed yourself.

If you do not already have a Nikon lens, probably the two least expensive lenses to get for it

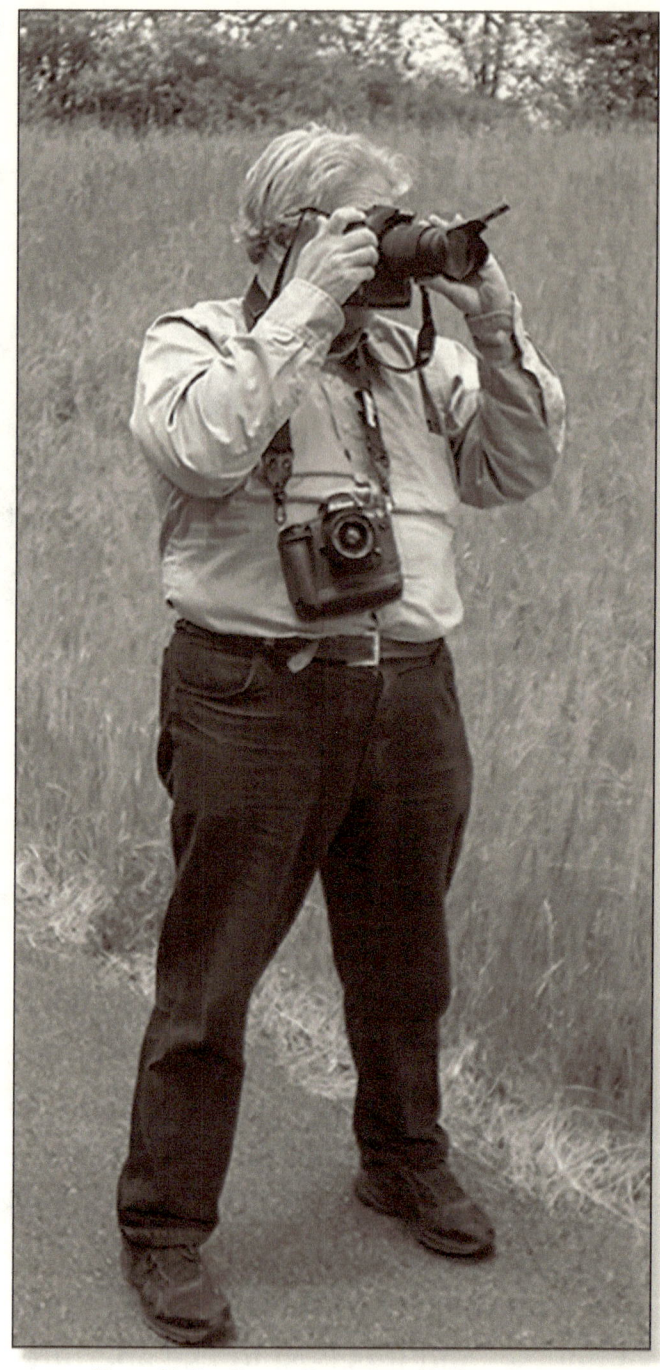

Shawn M. Tomlinson, Rotterdam, NY, May 31, 2014
Canon EOS 10D, 28mm, 1/1000, f/4, ISO 200, S, spot metering
© 2014 by Gary W. Ziroli

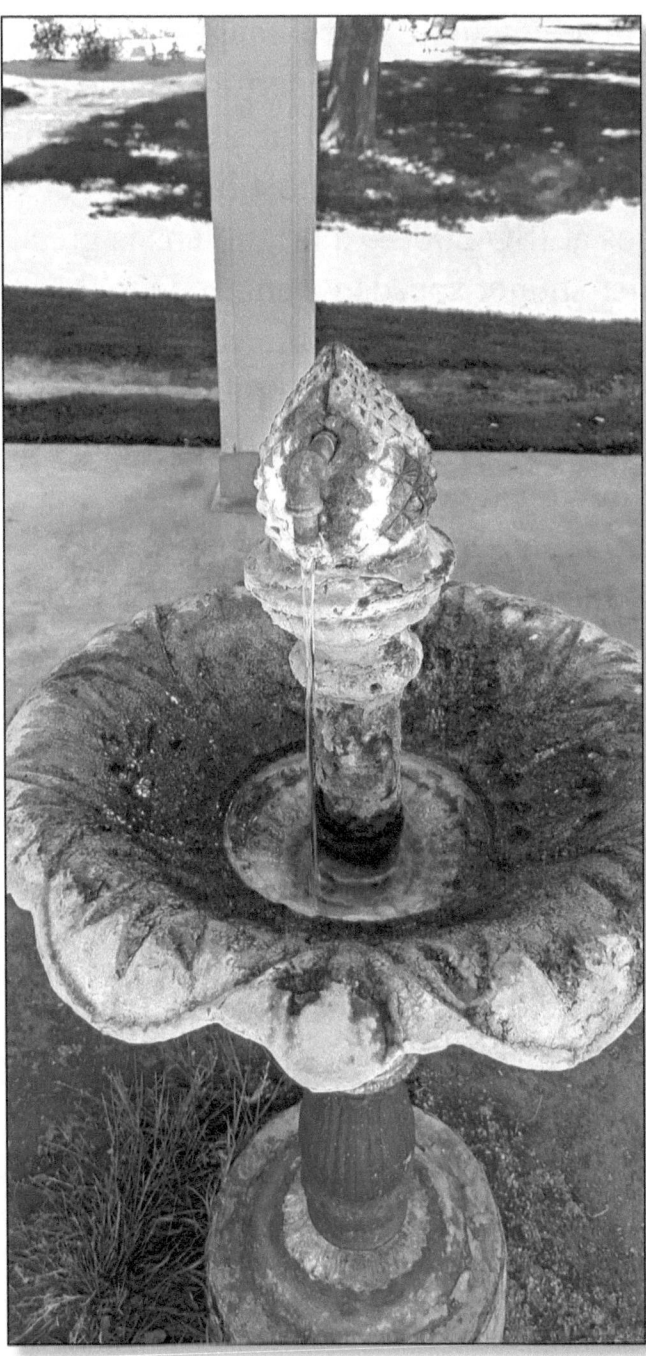

— one or the other — are the Nikon G DX 18-55mm f/3.5-5.6 or the Nikon AF D 50mm f/1.8.

The 18-55mm is known as a "kit" lens because it often is sold with entry-level DSLRs. It is a good all-around and versatile lens, but not the sharpest.

The 50mm lens,

a prime, will give you quite sharp images and has the bonus of a bright maximum aperture. Since you really won't be able to use the D1 at anything higher than ISO 400 — and you are most likely to get the best images at ISO 200 — a bright lens is great. It allows higher shutter speeds when needed.

If you want to be able to have the versatility of a zoom lens, than the 18-55mm definitely is your lens. If you don't mind physically moving yourself, the 50mm is much better.

I'm suggesting these lenses because they keep the budget for the D1 down. If you want to spend more, it's almost impossible to spend too much on a good lens. The better then lens, the better the images.

But because both of these lenses are relatively cheap — about $60 for the 18-55mm and about $100 for the 50mm — they keep the cost of the whole package to around $200.

And that is a great bargain, an unbeatable bargain, when it comes to pro DSLRs. There is no other pro DSLR that sells as cheaply.

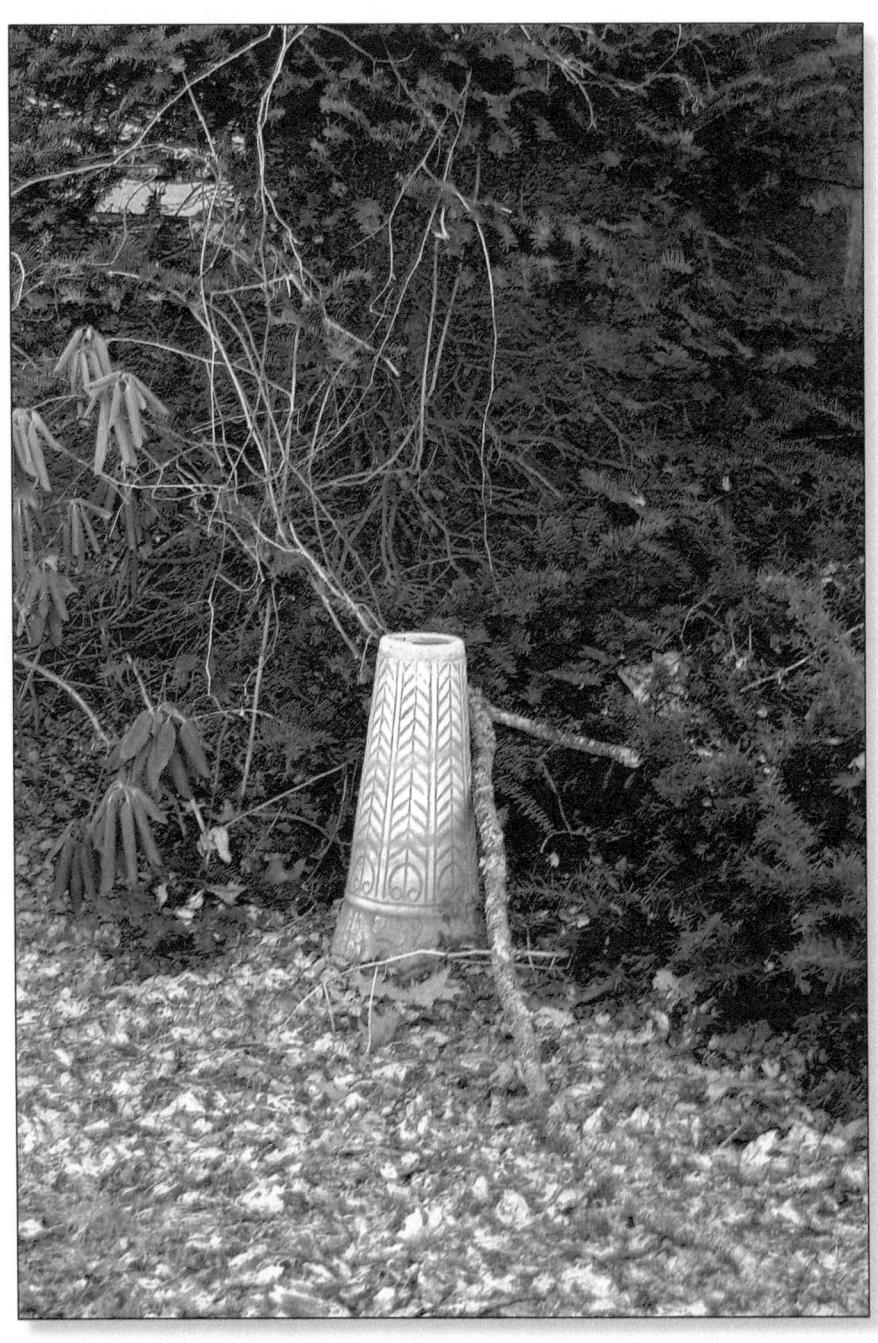

Ballston Lake, NY, April 2, 2014
Nikon D1, 66mm, 1/30, f/5.3, ISO 200, P, pattern metering
© 2014, 2015 by Shawn M. Tomlinson

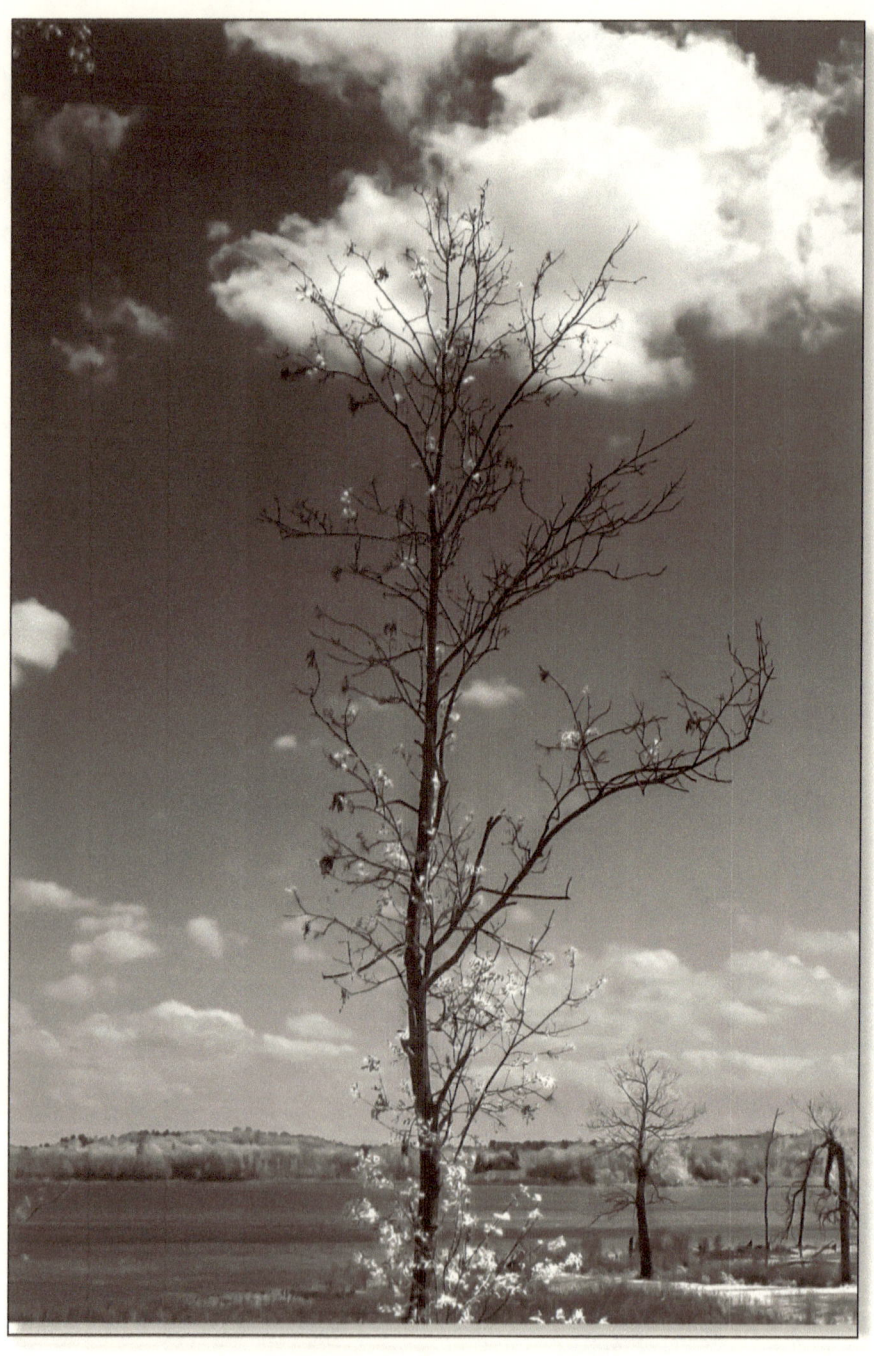

Round Lake, NY, May 17, 2014
Nikon D1, 38mm, 1/1500, f/5.6, ISO 200, Av, pattern metering
© 2014, 2015 by Shawn M. Tomlinson

Last Words

An ancient professional DSLR such as the Nikon D1 isn't for everyone. The average person who wants to take photos of their pets and post them on Instagram, for example, will find it annoying.

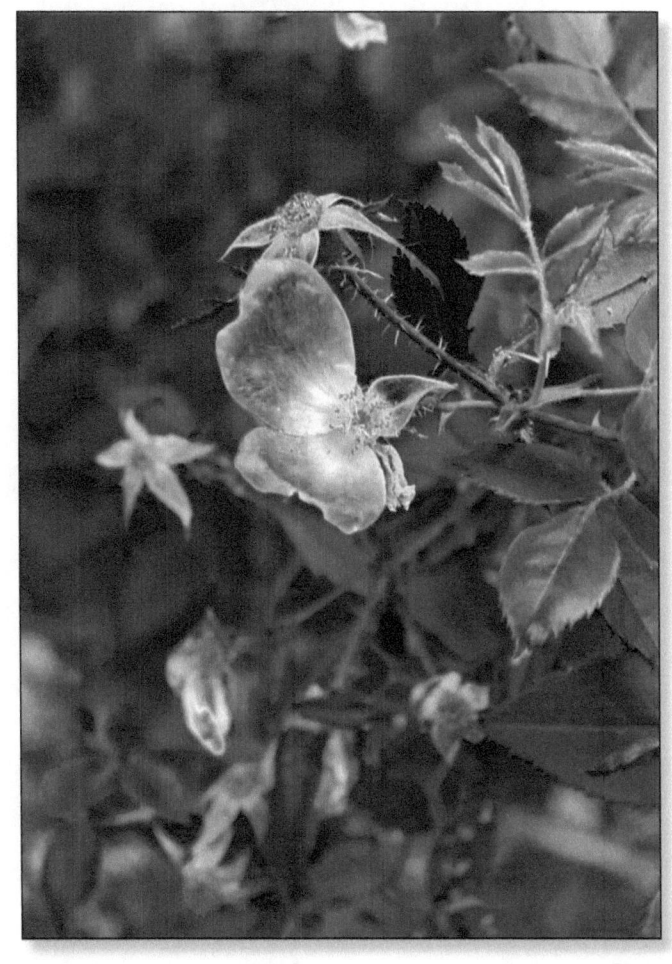

Saratoga Springs, NY, Dec. 13, 2014
Nikon D1, 55mm, 1/60, f/5.6, ISO 200, Av, pattern metering
© 2014 by Shawn M. Tomlinson

It really is for the photographer enthusiast who wants to know what its like to shoot with a pro DSLR but does not want to or cannot afford to pay the thousands of dollars required for a modern one.

The D1 these days is a quirky, fun, experimental DSLR camera that will give you lots of fun as an enthusiast without costing a lot.

And there's nothing wrong with that.

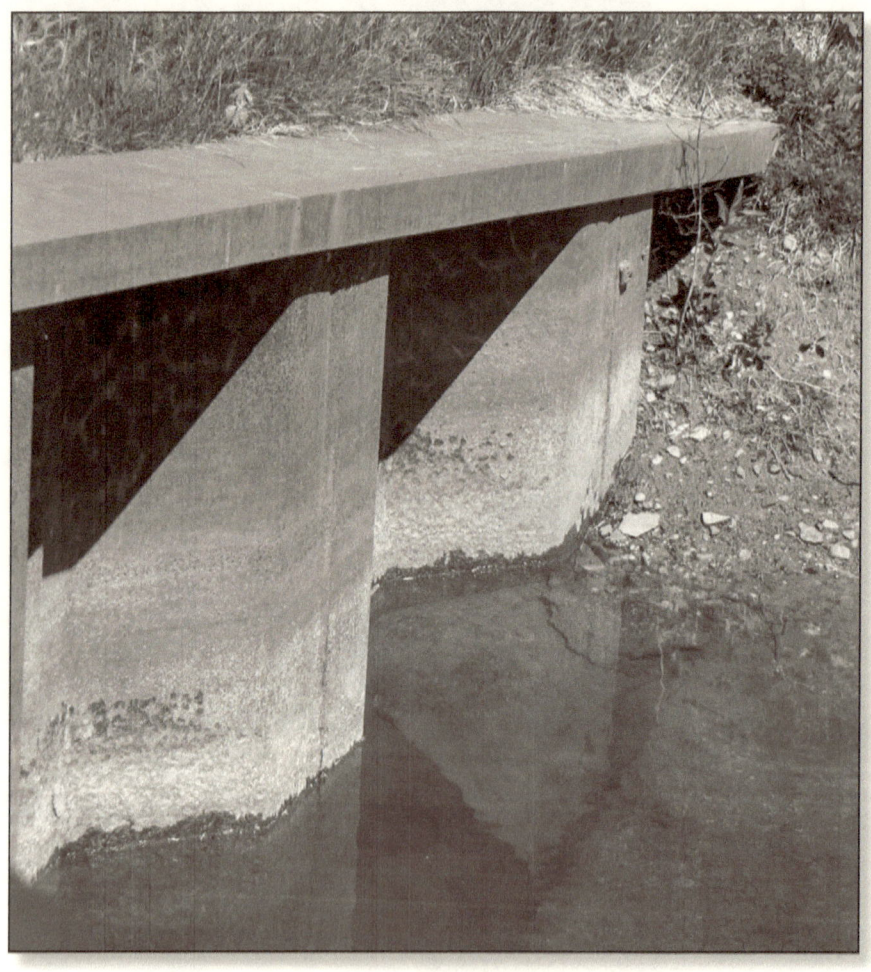

Round Lake, NY, May 17, 2014
Nikon D1, 80mm, 1/500, f/5.6, ISO 200, Av, pattern metering
© 2014, 2015 by Shawn M. Tomlinson

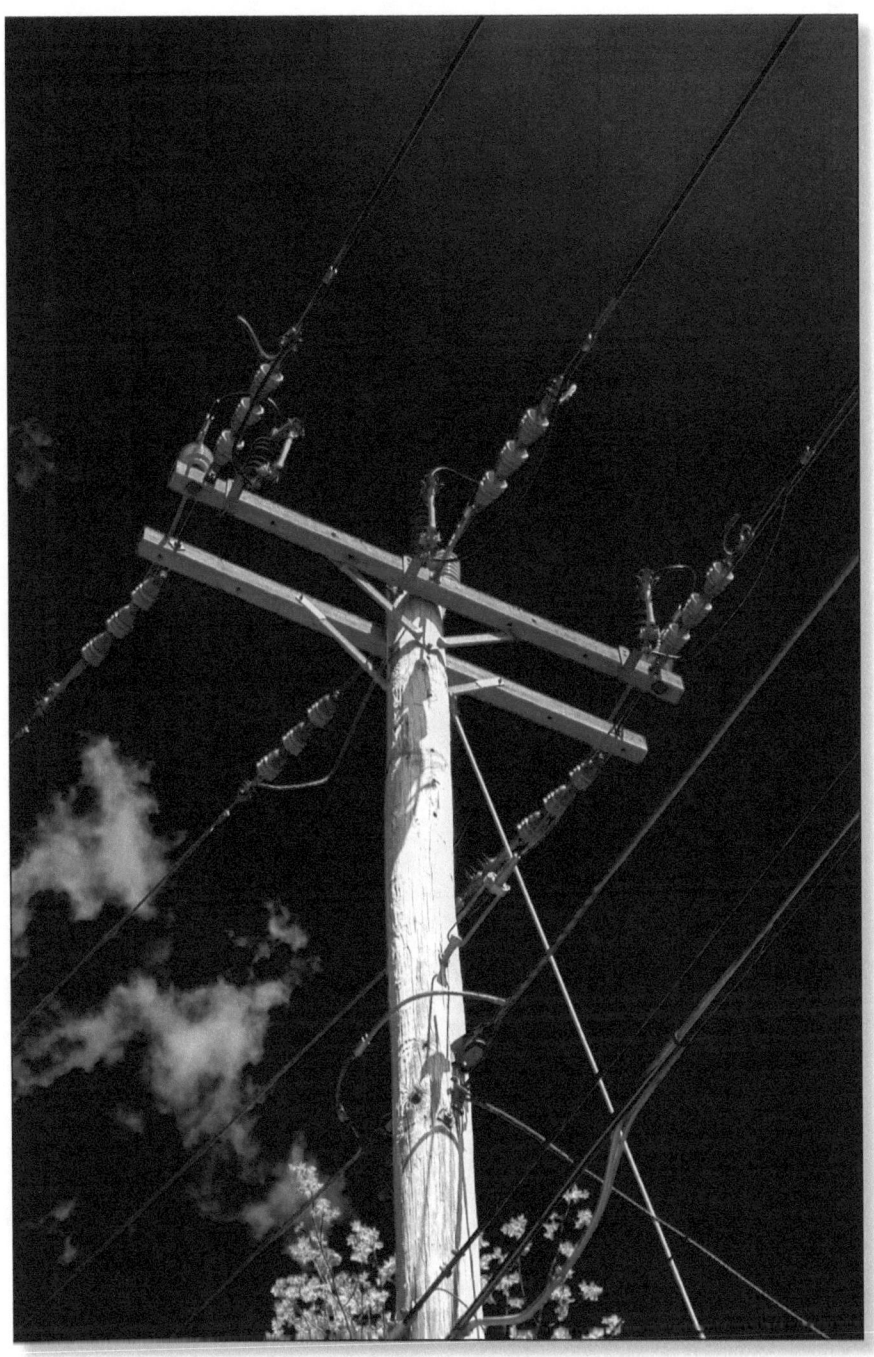

Round Lake, NY, May 17, 2014
Nikon D1, 48mm, 1/1000, f/5.6, ISO 200, Av, pattern metering
© 2014, 2015 by Shawn M. Tomlinson

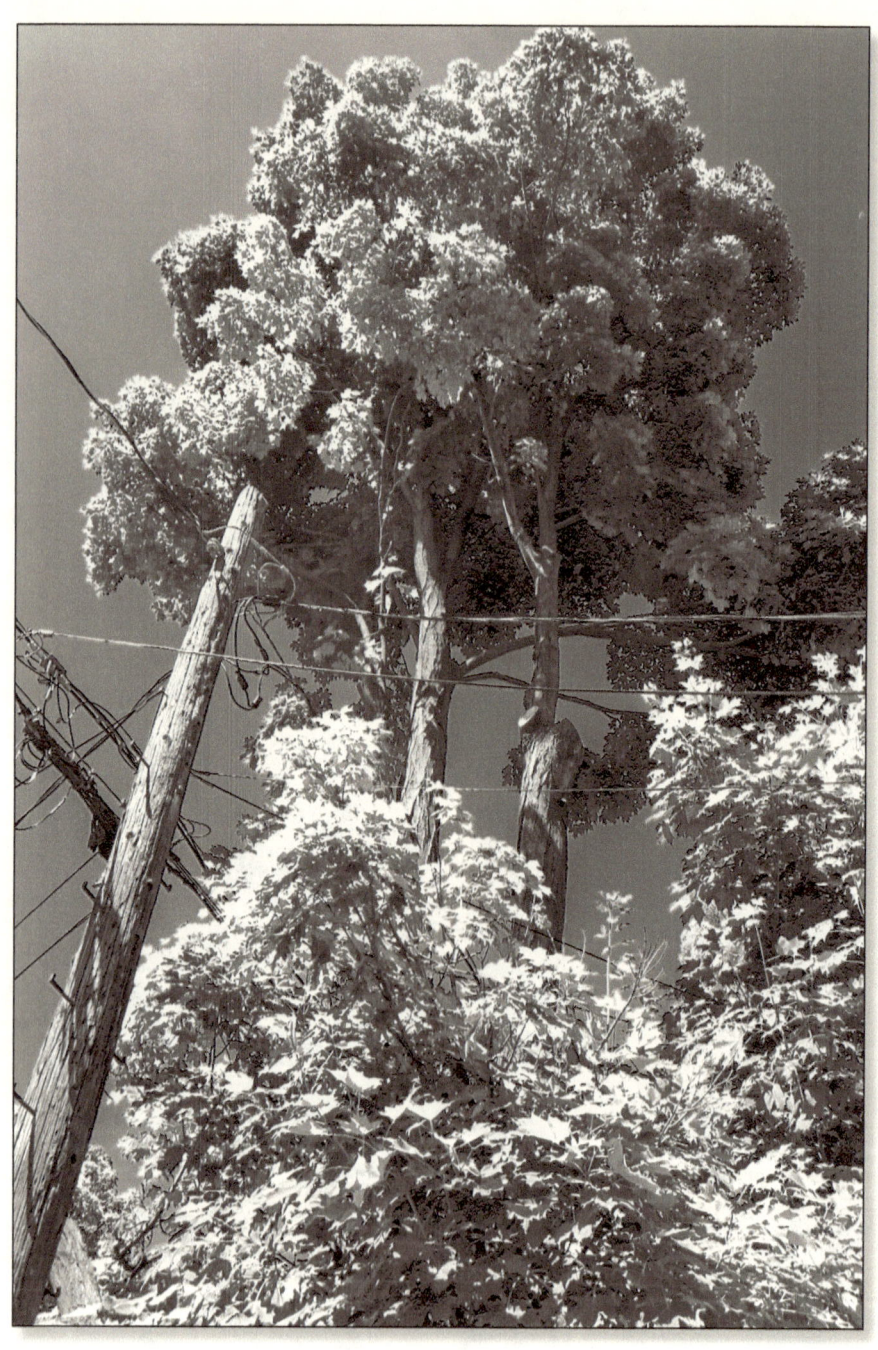

Saratoga Springs, NY, Aug. 19, 2014
Nikon D1, 18mm, 1/500, f/5.6, ISO 200, Av, pattern metering
© 2014 by Shawn M. Tomlinson

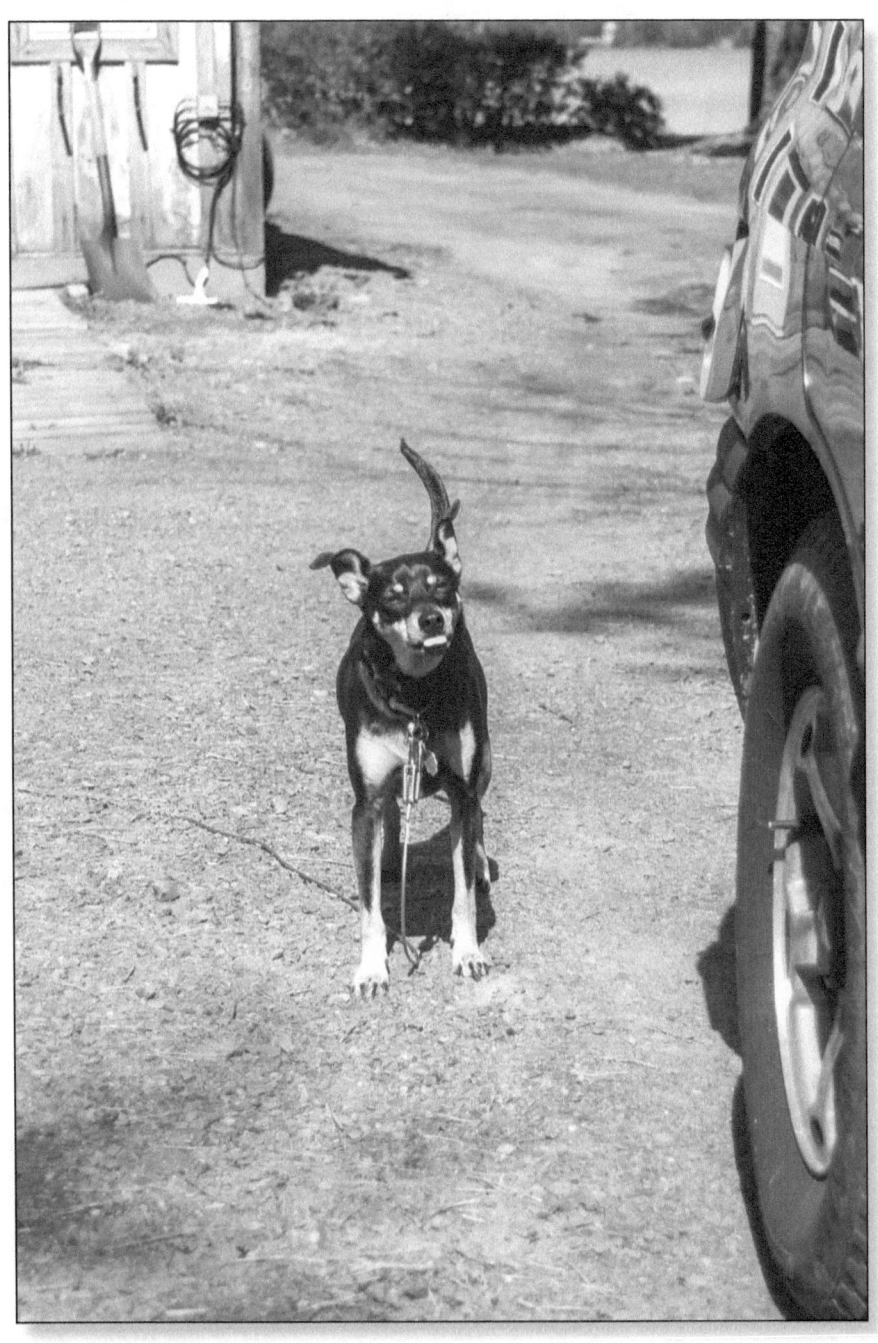

Oscar, Caroga Lake, NY, May 20, 2014
Nikon D1, 75mm, 1/1600, f/5.6, ISO 400, Av, pattern metering
© 2014, 2015 by Shawn M. Tomlinson

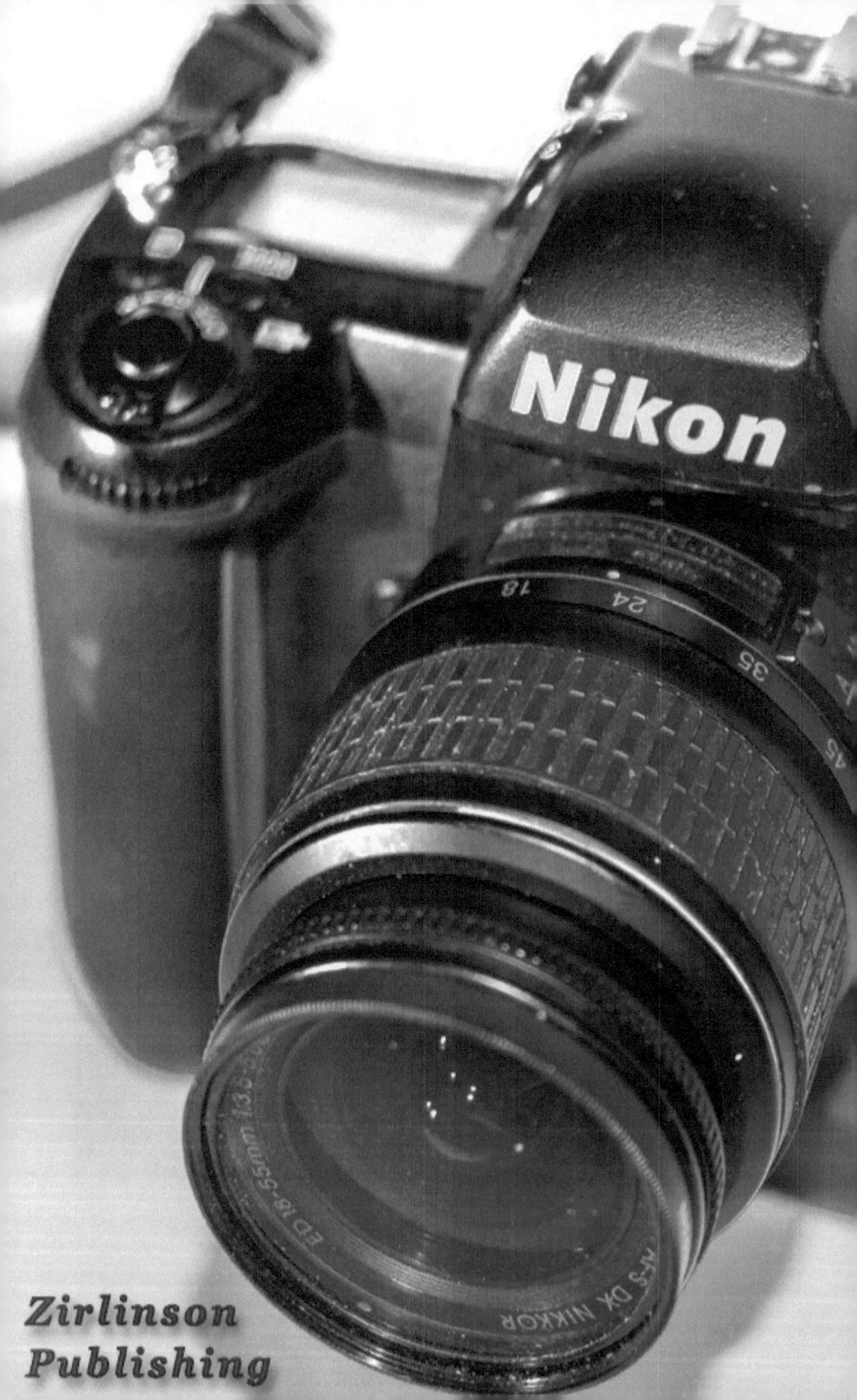

Zirlinson
Publishing

Volume 6: How to Choose a Prime Lens

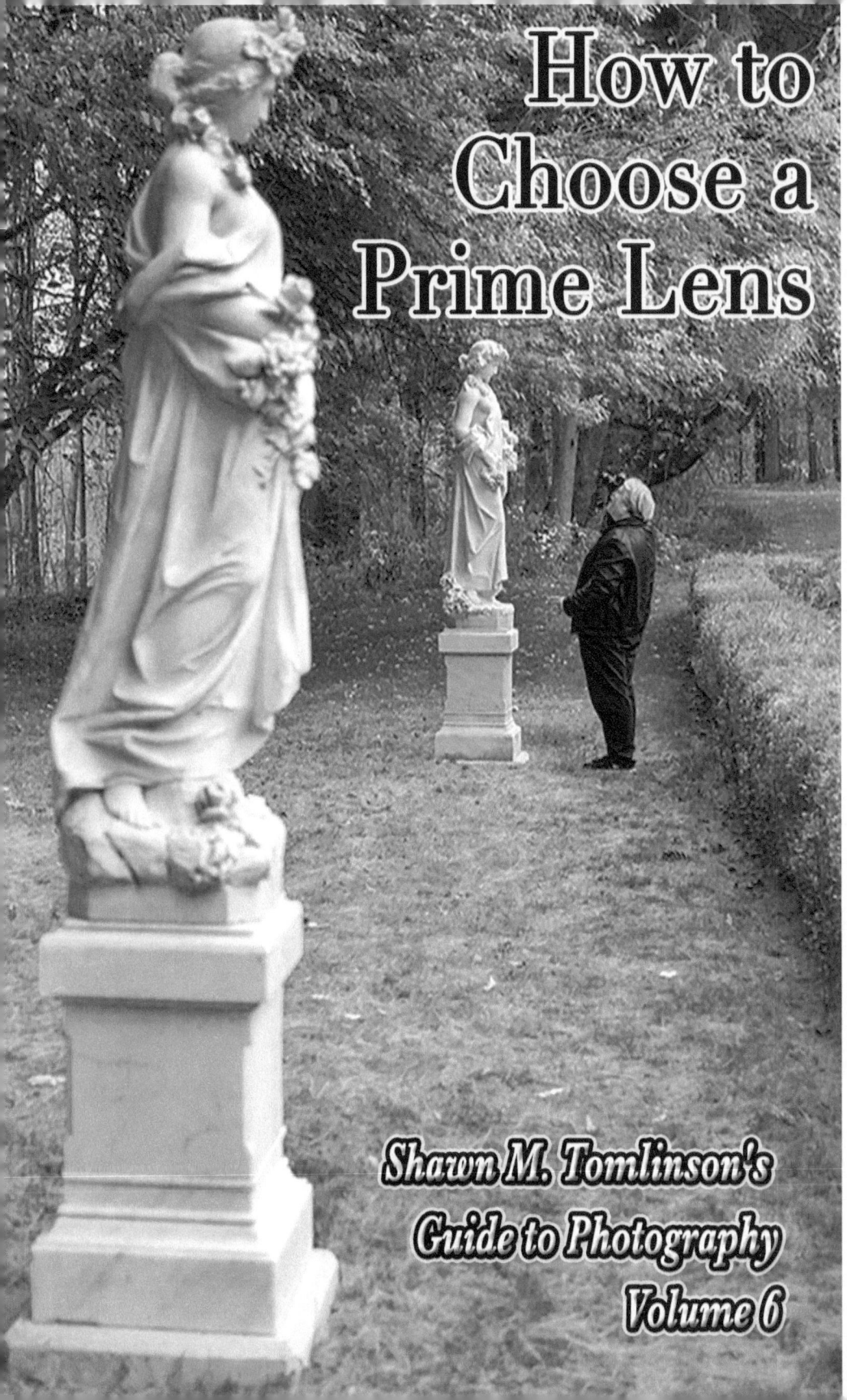

How to Choose a Prime Lens

How to Choose a Prime Lens

Shawn M. Tomlinson's
Guide to Photography
Volume 6

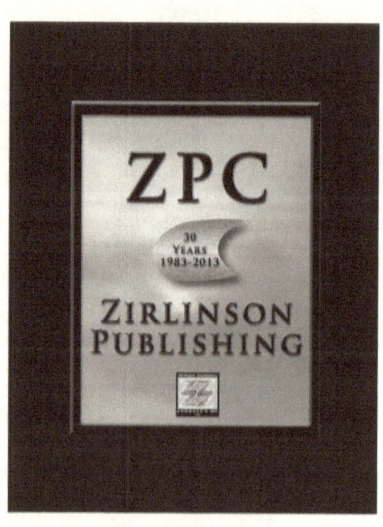

How to Choose a Prime Lens

Shawn M. Tomlinson's
Guide to Photography
Volume 6

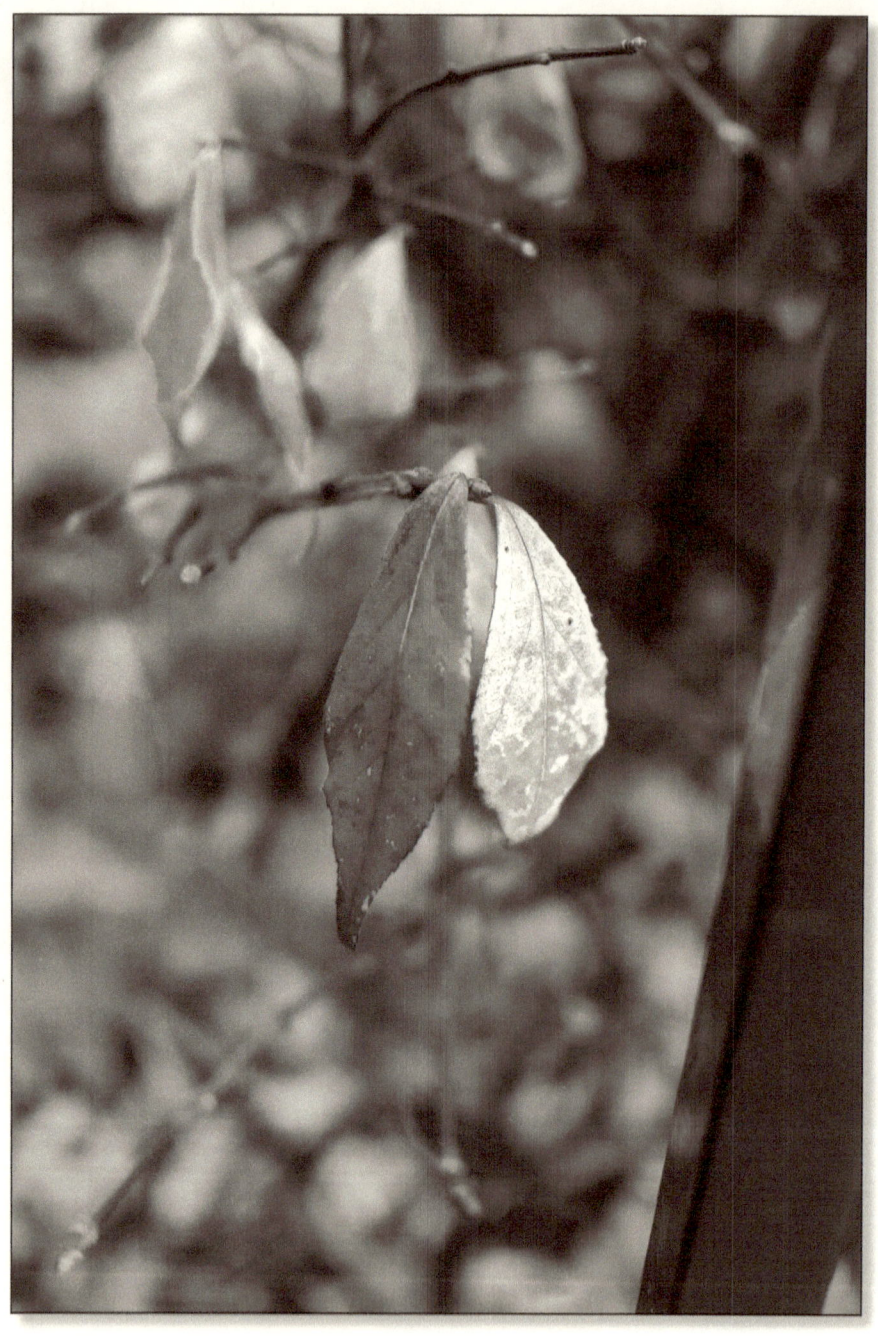

Saratoga Springs, N.Y., Nov. 25, 2014.
Nikon D7000, 28mm (prime), 1/1250, f/2.8, ISO 400, Tv, spot metering.
© 2014, 2015 by Shawn M. Tomlinson

Introduction

Prime lenses are making a comeback with amateur and professional photographers alike, and that's a good thing.

Sure, zoom lenses are easier, but they rarely have the sharpness, nor do they have the brightness, of prime or fixed-focal-length lenses. Primes do take a little more effort to use than zooms. You have to physically move closer or farther from your subject to make your composition, rather than just turning the zoom ring and letting the lens do it for you.

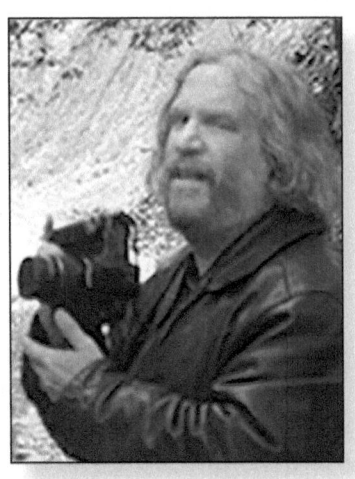

Shawn M. Tomlinson
© 2014, 2015 by Gary W. Ziroli

This slight change from what most photographers are used to now actually harkens back to the film days when prime lenses were the standard for most every single-lens reflex camera photographer.

In this short guide, I give you some pointers about what prime lenses do, what type you may need for your particular photographic vision and how to choose what you need.

Before we get started, just a little background.

I started with a 58mm prime lens on my first SLR camera, a Russian knock-off with the brand name Cosmorex on the camera and Cosmogon on the lens. I was 14 at the time and I used this camera for the next six years all the time. When it came time to move up to a bit better SLR and lens, it was the Pentax MX all manual SLR with a 50mm f/1.8 manual SMC Pentax lens.

I used this setup for all my early professional work and never thought much about the need for a zoom lens. That was until autofocus film SLRs came along. Suddenly, the old manual-focus zooms were a glut on the market and cheap. A year before, a 28-80mm manual zoom lens would have cost at least a couple of hundred dollars. When I bought it used, it was $50.

By the time I shifted to *my* first autofocus film SLR with the Pentax PZ-10, primes were considered things of the past, relics of a forgotten era. The new standard was the short zoom, usually 28-80mm or, for less money, the 35-70mm. For the PZ-10, I acquired a Sigma 35-80mm and an 80-200mm and never got a "standard" 50mm autofocus prime lens.

This concept continued into the digital age. Zooms were standard, and let's face it, had a lot better glass by then. Most people — other than a very few pros — did not use prime lenses.

This made primes expensive, but in recent years, prices have come down, at least for Canon and Nikon. Pentax primes — which are very good — still have high price tags.

And because the prices of primes started to drop and the quality of the glass got very good, even at the low prices, primes came back into style.

From about 1995 through 2014, I did not use a prime lens, except on the Pentax MX, with which I still shot occasionally, and still do. Oh, and I did try it on my Pentax K20D digital single-lens reflex camera with great results.

Then I switched brand loyalty for a variety of reasons and the opportunity arose for me to purchase a Nikon AF D 28mm f/2.8 lens for my several Nikon DSLRs, but primarily for my D7000. I had been worried I wouldn't like using a prime again, knew I needed one, but kept putting off the purchase for several years.

Once I put the 28mm lens on the D7000, well, I was in love again. I have used other lenses rarely in the month I've had the prime. Later, I decided the Nikon AF D 50mm f/1.8 was more to my liking, so I traded the 28mm for it with a friend. When finances permit, I either will reacquire a 28mm or get a 24mm. I just put in an order for the Nikon G VR 105mm micro lens, and honestly, I expect this to become, well, my prime prime.

And I never mind zooming my body rather than my lens.

— Shawn M. Tomlinson
July 4, 2015

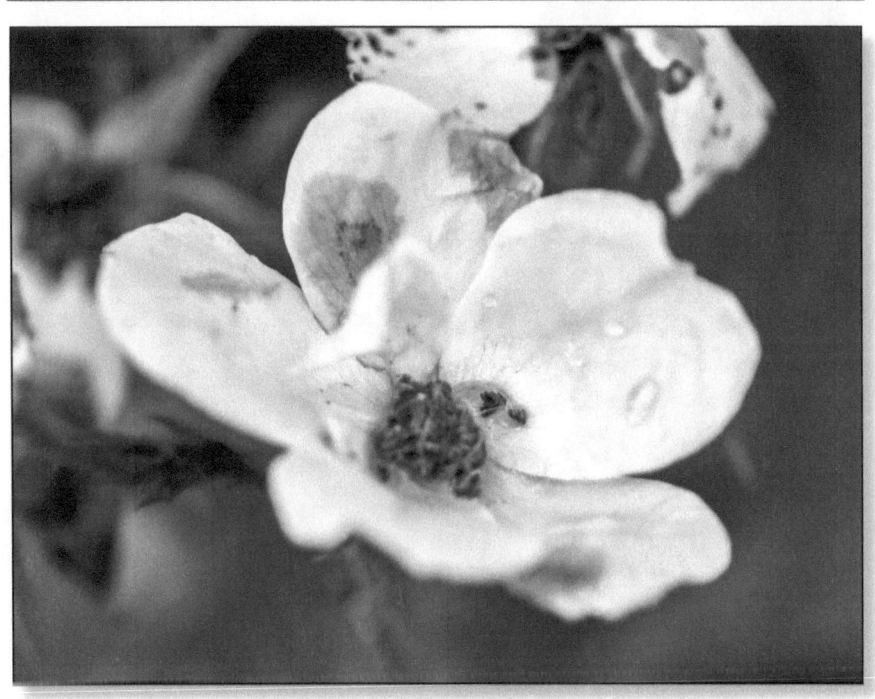

Ballston Lake, NY, July 10, 2015
Nikon D800e, 105mm, 1/400, f/3.2, ISO 200, S, pattern metering
© 2015 by Shawn M. Tomlinson

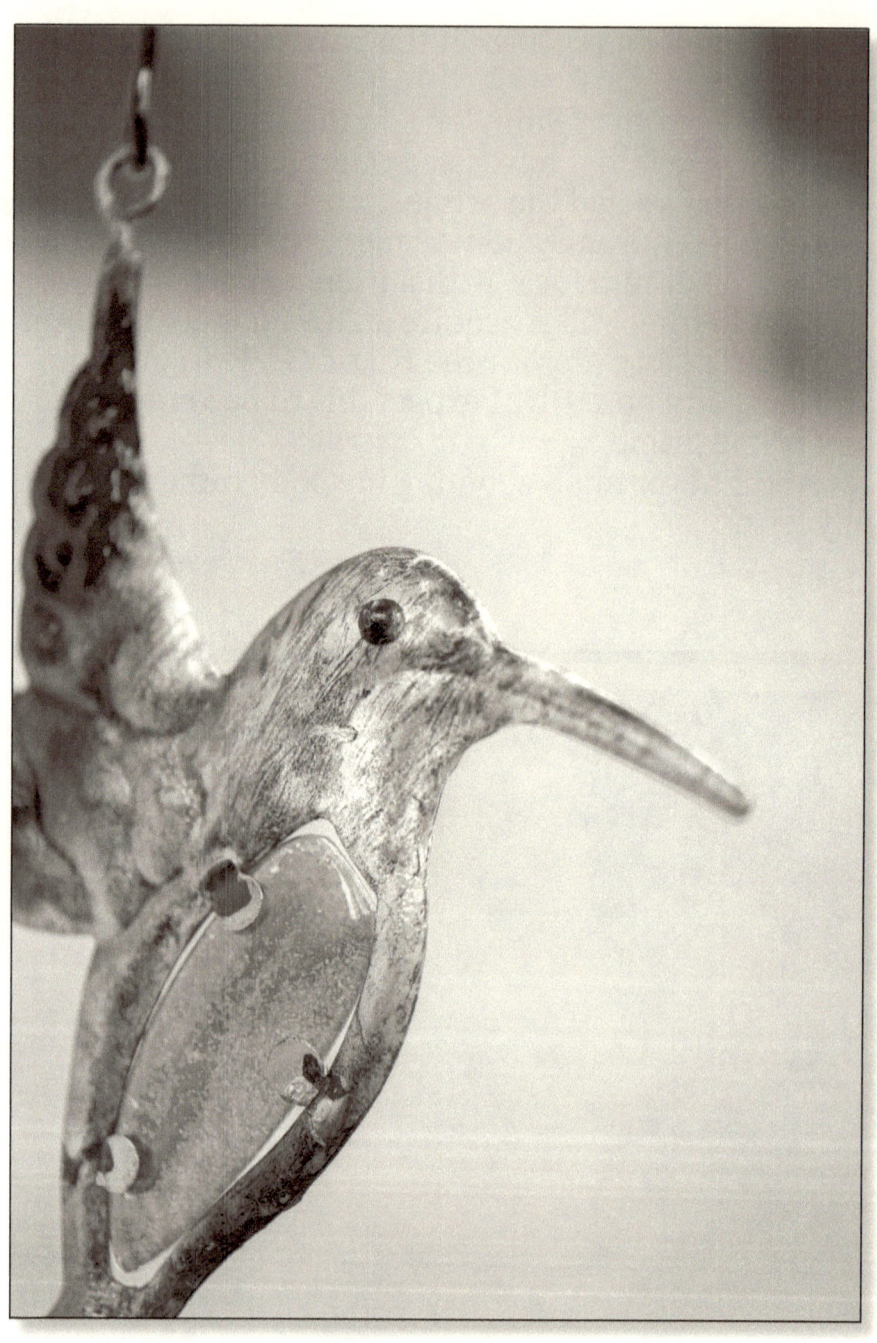

Ballston Lake, NY, July 9, 2015
Nikon D800e, 105mm, 1/200, f/4, ISO 200, S, pattern metering
© 2015 by Shawn M. Tomlinson

Starting Points

I am assuming for this book that you are using an APS-C or crop-frame sensor digital single-lens reflex camera. My calculations are based upon the 1.5x crop factor of the Nikon, Pentax and Sony DSLRs and the 1.6x crop factor of the Canon cameras.

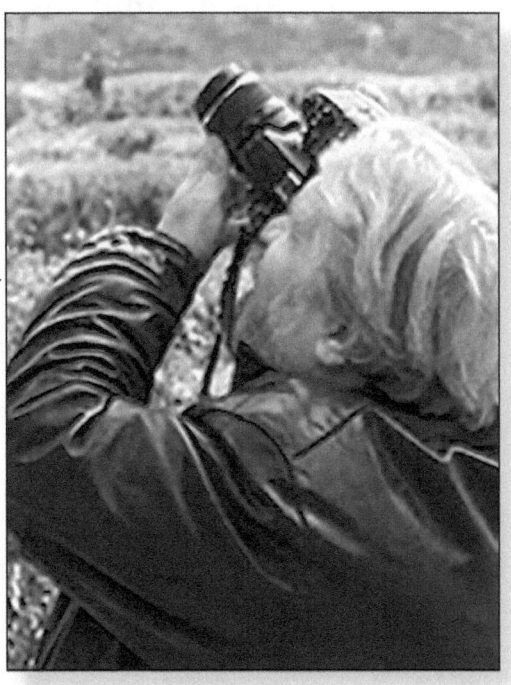

Shawn M. Tomlinson
© 2014 by Gary W. Ziroli

If you have a full-frame DSLR, more power to you. I like them, but decided to stay with the APS-C format for now when I traded in the full-frame Canon EOS 1DS for the crop-frame Nikon D7000. I went back to full frame with the Nikon D800e, but continue to shoot with the D7000 and a Nikon D2x. For non-pro photographers, the APS-C DSLRs are more common than full frame, mostly because they are cheaper. And, because APS-C cameras are getting better constantly, more pros are using them, too, at least as second or backup DSLR bodies.

The lenses I am mentioning all work on APS-C cameras, but not all work on full-frame DSLRs. The best thing about the full-frame cameras in relation to these lenses is that you do not have to make any calculations to figure out the actual focal length. What's written on the lens is what it is. A 24mm lens on a full-frame DSLR is really 24mm, not the 36mm it is on a Nikon or the 38.4mm on the Canon.

Except for these angle-of-view considerations, this guide works for both types of DSLRs.

However, you must be careful when buying because manufacturers have two sets of lenses, one for full-frame and one for crop-frame cameras. Nikon designates its APS-C-only lenses as DX and its full-frame lenses as FX. Canon's crop-frame-only lenses are designated as EF-S and its full-frame lenses as EF.

You can use full-frame lenses on crop-frame cam-

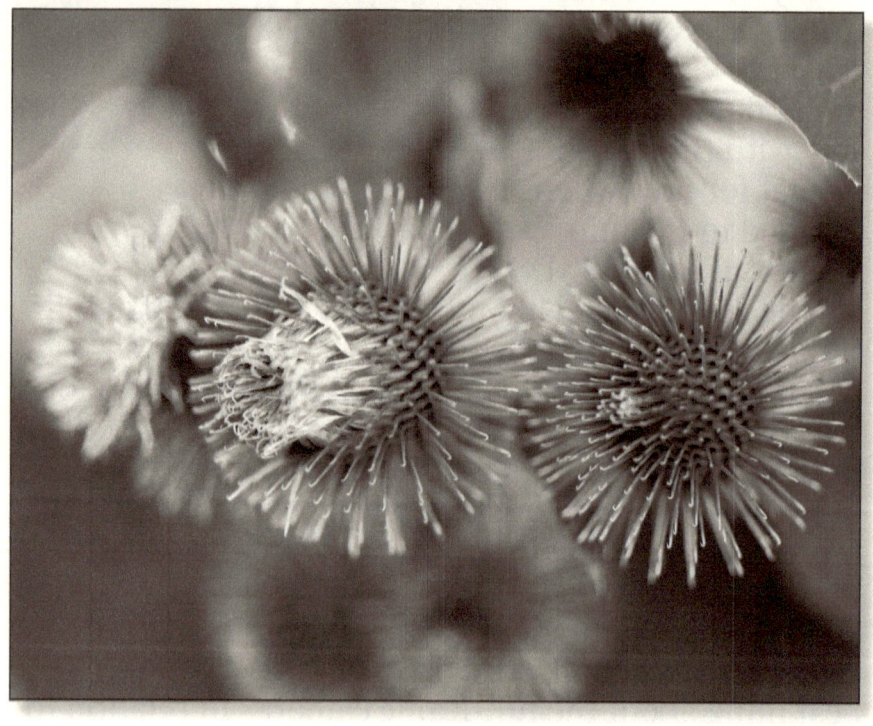

Riverside Park, Schenectady, NY, July 10, 2015
Nikon D800e, 105mm, 1/640, f/3.2, ISO 200, S, pattern metering
© 2015 by Shawn M. Tomlinson

eras, but you can't use crop-frame lenses on full-frame cameras in most cases. A Nikon FX lens works on full-frame and crop-frame DSLRs, but a Nikon DX lens will produce black corners on a full-frame camera because it isn't designed to cover the full area of the bigger sensor.

The exception, at least with Nikon, is that its DSLRs allow the photographer to use DX lenses on FX cameras by the use of an "Image Area" menu item.

How this works is that there is a separate rectangle within the viewfinder to show the DX area. As long as you keep the subject composition within that area, you won't get the black corners. You'll still see them

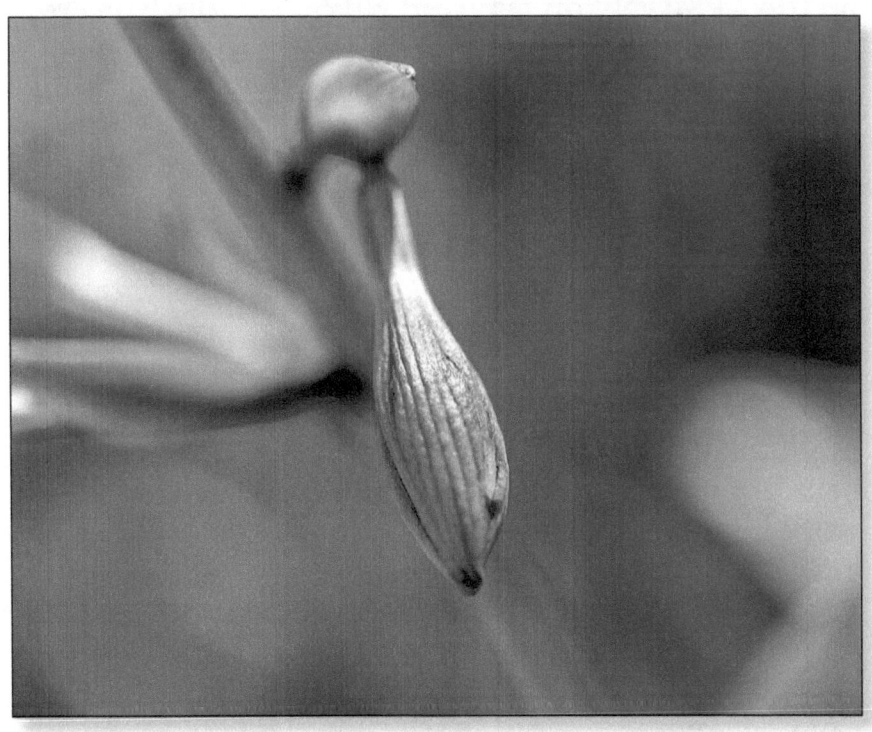

Riverside Park, Schenectady, NY, July 10, 2015
Nikon D800e, 105mm, 1/1000, f/4.5, ISO 200, S, pattern metering
© 2015 by Shawn M. Tomlinson

in the viewfinder, but you won't on the LCD display.

This in-camera cropping does cut down the resolution. So, for example, if I shoot with an FX lens, such as the Nikon AF D 50mm f/1.8 on the D800e, I get 36.2-megapixel resolution. If I shoot with the Nikon G 18-55mm kit lens, I get 16-megapixel resolution. And, of course, the image quality is not as good simply because the kit lens is not as good optically as the 50mm prime.

Nikon has allowed the use of DX lenses on its full-frame cameras since the introduction of its first one, the pro Nikon D3.

In my case, this is particularly useful with the Sigma DC 10-20mm f/4-5.6 ultra-wide zoom. This is a very good, sharp lens that produces fantastic images on the APS-C Nikon D2x and Nikon D7000. The crop factor makes it 15-30mm on these cameras.

I now use it, too, on the D800e because — as long as I remember to switch the "Image Area" to DX — it produces images of about the same quality as the D7000.

Nikon FX DSLRs switch the "Image Area" automatically for Nikon-manufactured lenses, but for third-party lenses such as the aforementioned Sigma, it must be done manually.

As far as I know, however, prime lenses only are manufactured as full-frame lenses, so choosing any prime will work now on your APS-C camera, and also work later on your full-frame camera, if you choose to get one.

Remember, though, that the crop factor still exists on APS-C DSLRs, so that 50mm prime lens equals 75mm on Nikon, Pentax and Sony, and 80mm on Canon cameras.

Canon simply does not let full-frame lenses to be

used on its crop-frame cameras. It physically prevents EF-S lenses from mounting on full-frame cameras.

If you have any intention of eventually moving to full-frame, do not buy crop-frame or so-called "digital" lenses for your Canon, unless you are prepared to buy replacement full-frame lenses later.

There's actually nothing wrong with having both types of lenses if you plan to use both APS-C and full-frame cameras like I do.

Of course, the manufacturers put the most effort and quality into their full-frame lenses, so buy the full-frame lenses if possible.

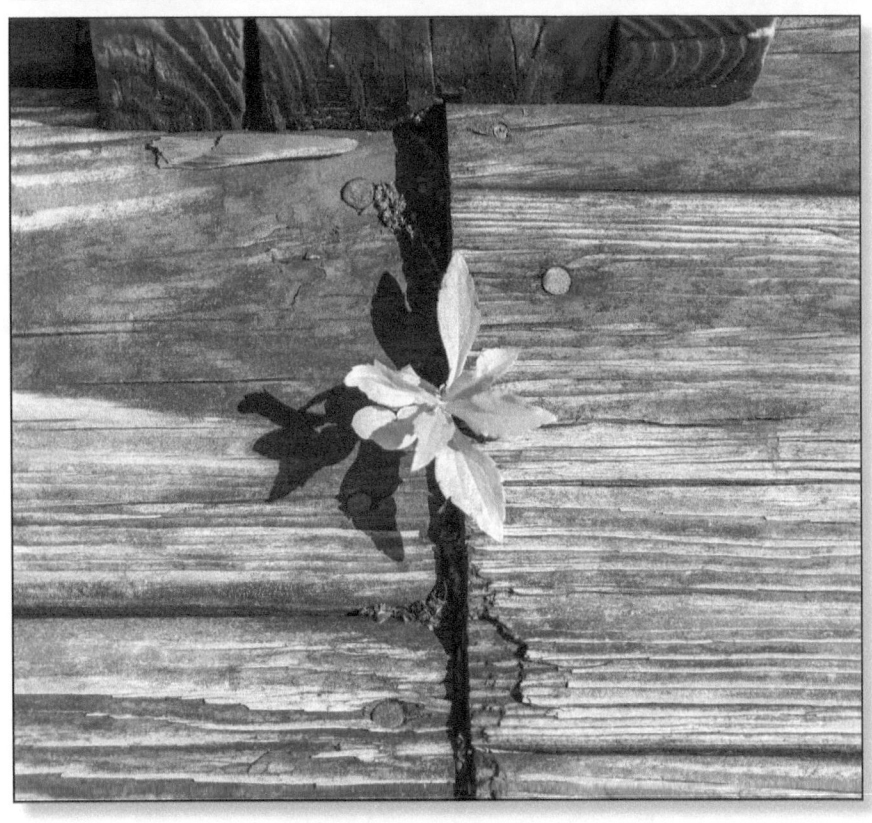

Gateway Park, Schenectady, NY, July 10, 2015
Nikon D800e, 105mm, 1/400, f/8, ISO 200, S, pattern metering
© 2015 by Shawn M. Tomlinson

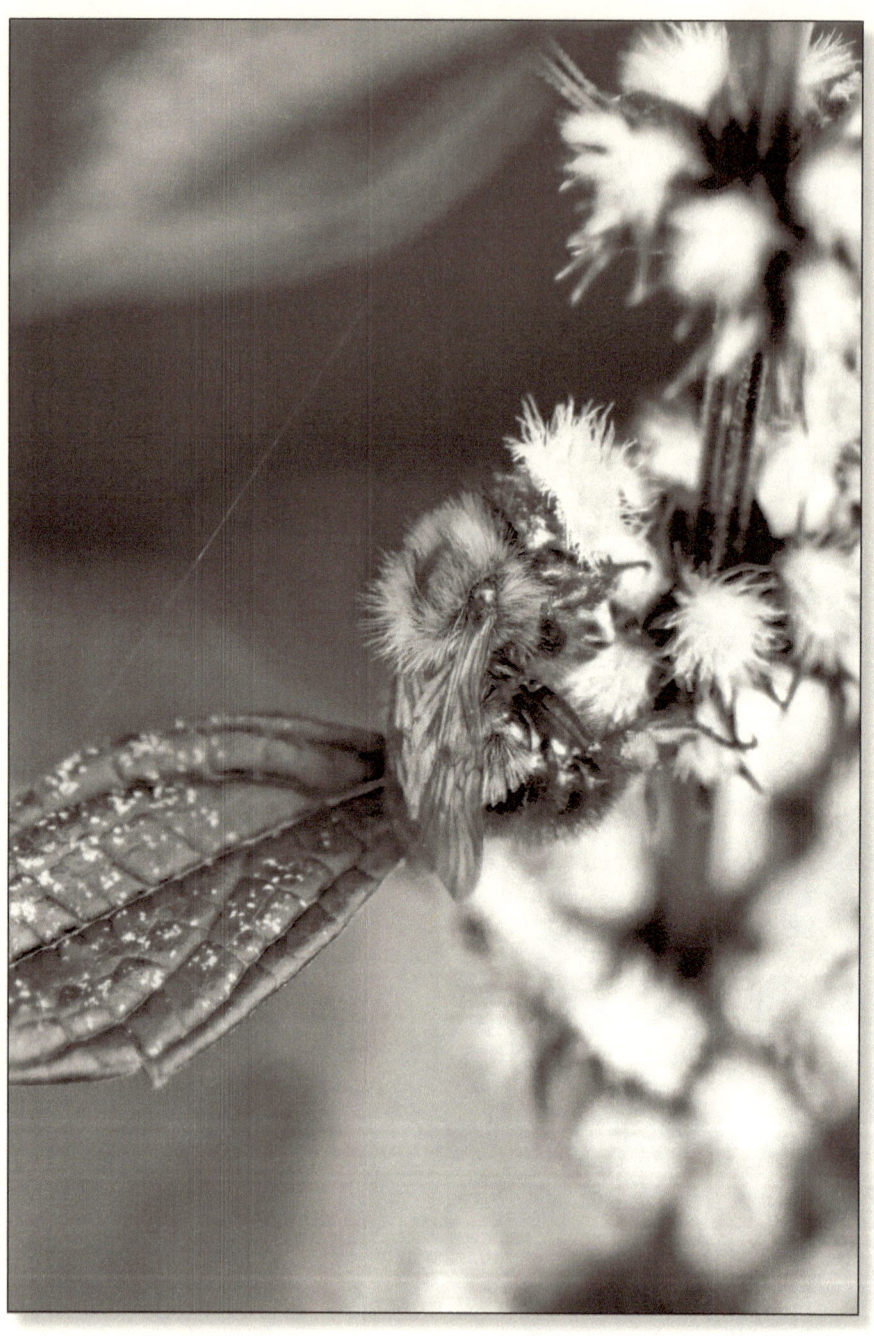

Riverside Park, Schenectady, NY, July 10, 2015
Nikon D800e, 105mm, 1/640, f/3.2, ISO 200, S, pattern metering
© 2015 by Shawn M. Tomlinson

How to Choose a Prime Lens

PART 1: BRANDS

It used to be that third-party lenses never were quite as good as those made by the same people who made the camera.

So, Nikon cameras needed Nikon lenses, Canon needed Canon, etc.

This still is true to a great extent, but Sigma is challenging the big-name lens makers with its "art" series of lenses.

Comparison shots I've seen so far give a very good case for buying these lenses.

The problem is that, the main motivation in buying third-party lenses usually is price.

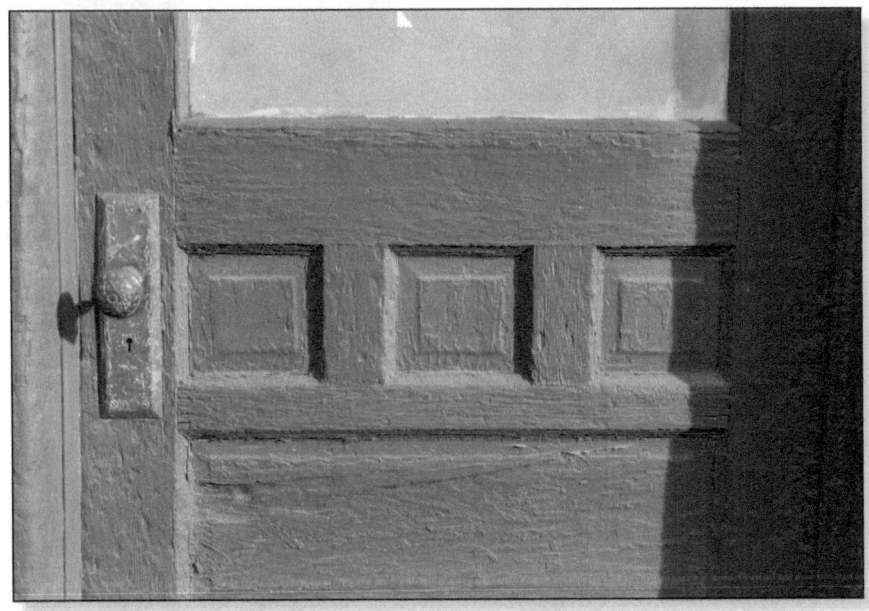

Saratoga Springs, N.Y., Nov. 25, 2014.
Nikon D7000, 28mm (prime), 1/1250, f/2.8, ISO 400, S, spot metering.
© 2014, 2015 by Shawn M. Tomlinson

They cost less.

A Sigma 18-200mm "travel" lens will cost, especially used, about a third of the cost of a Nikon, Canon, Pentax or Minolta/Sony lens. These new Sigma prime lenses, though, do not present significant savings, so I have to wonder why anyone would buy them instead of comparably priced original manufacturer lenses.

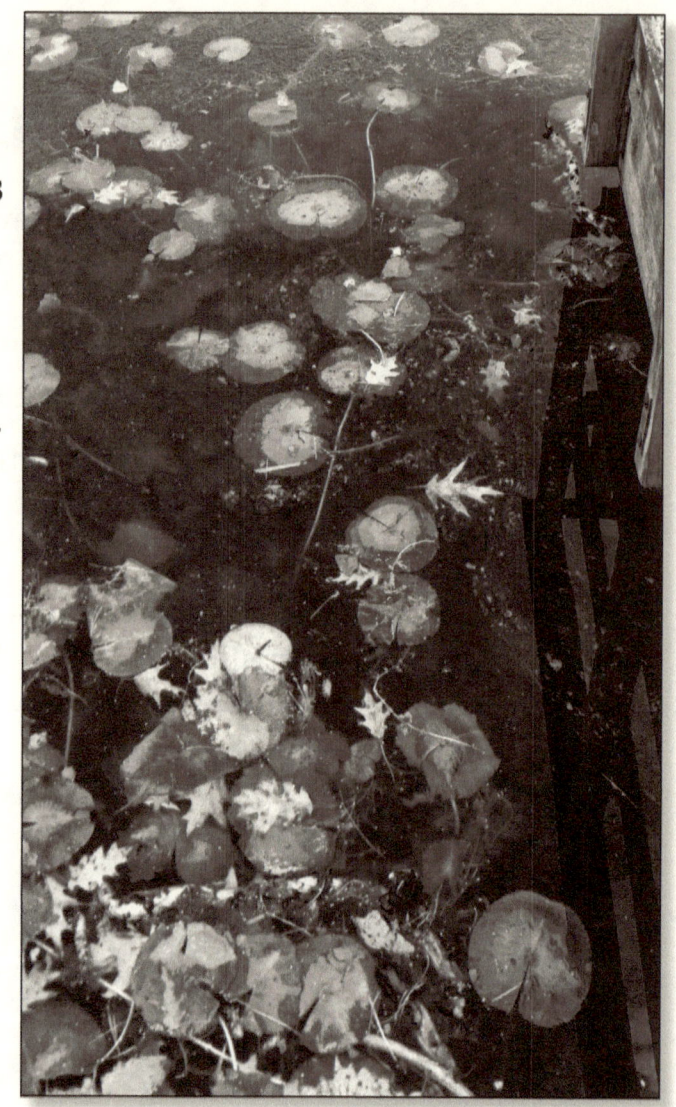

Ballston Lake, N.Y., Nov. 23, 2014.
Nikon D7000, 28mm (prime), 1/500, f/2.8, ISO 400, S, spot metering.
© 2014, 2015 by Shawn M. Tomlinson

Sigma, Tamron and Tokina — the three main third-party lens makers, and the only ones for a se-

rious pho-
tographer
to even
remotely
consider
— do not
make that
many prime
lenses. They
tend to
specialize in
zooms, be-
cause their
strategists
figure most
pros — the
people who
buy most of
the prime
lenses — ar-
en't going
to consider
third-party
lenses for
their work.
For
prime
lenses, the
truth is that
with the
exception

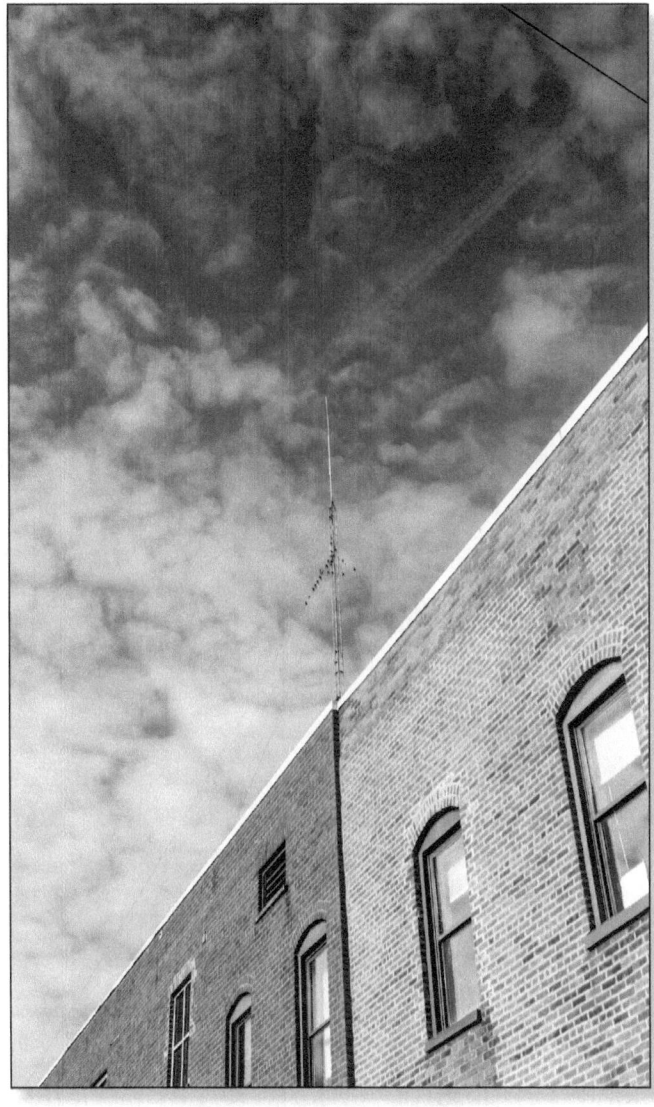

Saratoga Springs, N.Y., Nov. 25, 2014.
Nikon D7000, 28mm (prime), 1/2000, f/5.6, ISO 250, S, spot metering.
© 2014, 2015 by Shawn M. Tomlinson

of Pentax, the manufacturers make really good ones glass-wise that may not be as good otherwise for not much money.

For example, Canon's 50mm f/1.8 EF STM lens

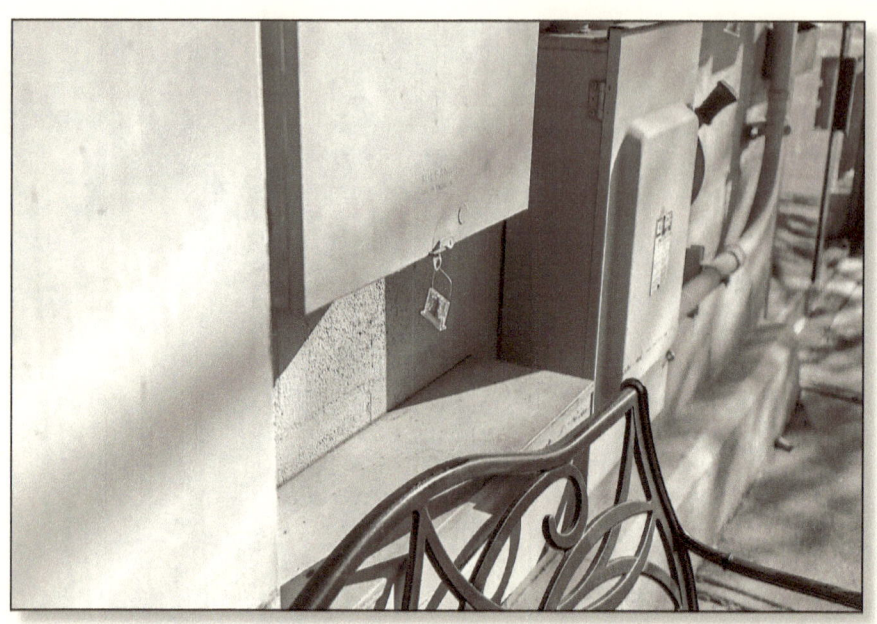

Saratoga Springs, N.Y., Nov. 22, 2014.
Nikon D7000, 28mm (prime), 1/2000, f/2.8, ISO 250, S, spot metering.
© 2014, 2015 by Shawn M. Tomlinson

retails for $125. The body is plastic and not that durable, but the glass is just as sharp as much more expensive lenses. This newer version of the old standby 50mm EF II lens does have a metal mount, though, so that makes it a little more stable.

Nikon's AF D 50mm f/1.8 lens lists for $135 and has great glass quality. Pentax's 50mm f/1.8 has a much higher retail price of $250, but it is weather sealed and better built than either Canon's or Nikon's basic prime 50mm lens. Sony's 50mm Alpha Mount f/1.8 prime lists for $169.

Of course, buying used photographic equipment, including prime lenses, from reputable dealers — KEH.com especially — will bring those prices down significantly.

This is particularly true with Sony because the company's DSLR line is based upon technology and patents it bought when Konica-Minolta ceased making cameras.

Any lens with Minolta Maxxum written on it or that states it is for the Minolta/Sony Alpha Mount will work on Sony DSLRs. Although prices change frequently, just as an example, I paid $45 for a Minolta Maxxum 50mm f/1.7 lens from KEH. It produces stunning photographs

And, although Minolta may appear as a third-party lens for Sony, it isn't. Minolta was a great camera maker for many years and its products were of high quality.

Note that Minolta, like Canon, changed its lens mount when it moved from manual to autofocus. This means that without an expensive adapter, manual-focus Minolta and Canon lenses do not work on DSLRs. Nikon and Pentax manual-focus lenses made starting in the mid-1970s do work on their cameras.

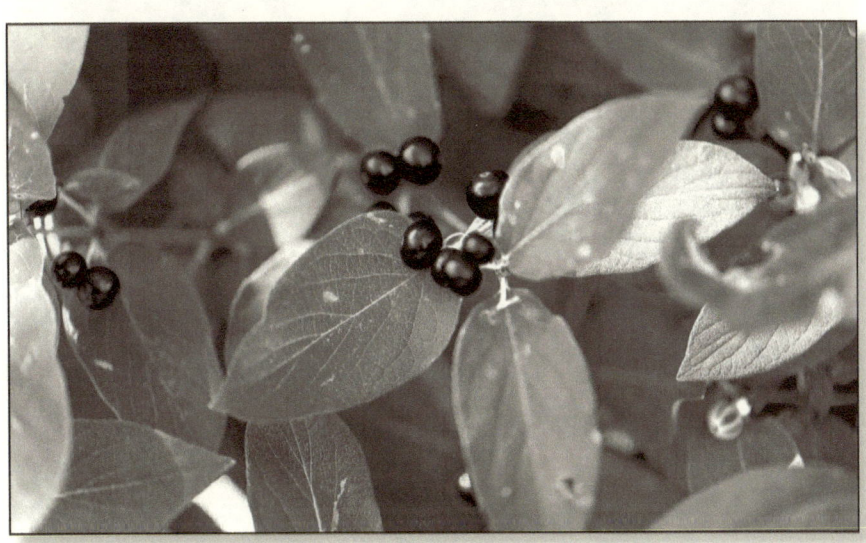

Riverside Park, Schenectady, NY, July 10, 2015
Nikon D800e, 105mm, 1/1000, f/3.2, ISO 200, S, pattern metering
© 2015 by Shawn M. Tomlinson

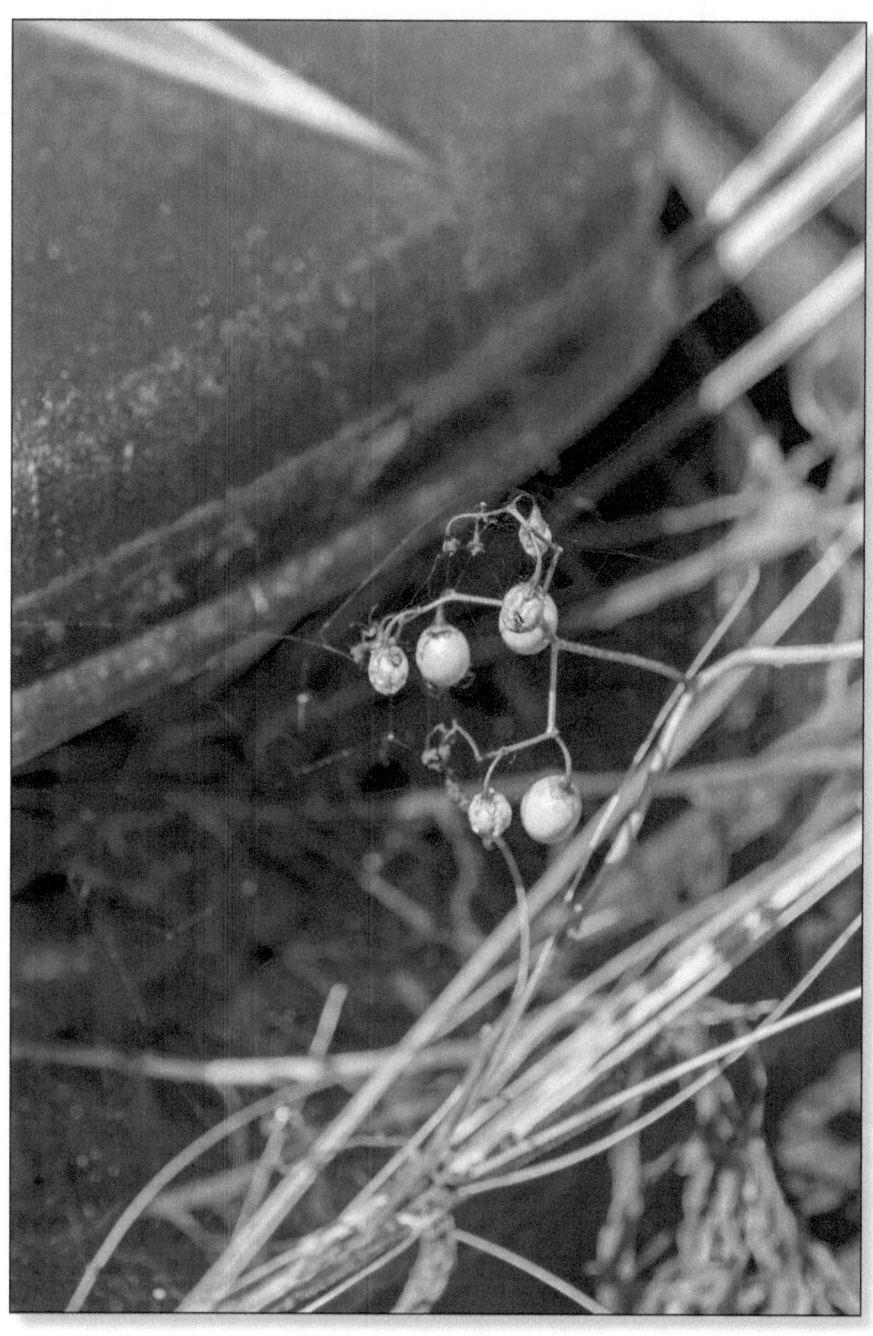

Ballston Lake, NY, July 10, 2015
Nikon D800e, 105mm, 1/200, f/9, ISO 400, S, pattern metering
© 2015 by Shawn M. Tomlinson

PART 2: FOCAL LENGTH

I've been talking largely about 50mm primes to this point because they once were the standard.

On a film SLR or a full-frame DSLR, 50mm lenses have the same effective focal length as your eyes. If you hold the camera to your eye, compose the scene and take the camera away from your eye, you see the same thing. The subject and surroundings are the same size through the lens and without it.

This changed when DSLR manufacturers opted for the cheaper APS-C or crop-frame sensors for their cameras. Nikon and Canon made their first pro DSLRs with these smaller sensors and the trend continued. Kodak made full-frame sensor cameras, but shut the line down a few years before filing for bankruptcy.

The result of these smaller-than-35mm-film-frame sensors was that they effectively cut the angle of view on all lenses, making them appear to be less wide-angle and more telephoto. To keep track of this, photographers multiply their lens focal lengths by the crop factor.

In other words, Nikon, Pentax and Sony have a crop factor of 1.5x and Canon has 1.6x in their APS-C DSLRs. This means that a 50mm lens becomes 75mm (50 x 1.5 = 75) with a Nikon, Pentax or Sony APS-C DSLR, and it becomes 80mm (50 x 1.6 = 80) with a Canon.

So a 50mm lens no longer gives you the same view you see with your eyes on this type of camera, but instead gives the slight telephoto of a Portrait lens.

The crop factor has some advantages. For example,

because it pushes the 50mm out to portrait length, it produces blurry backgrounds known as bokeh, an effect often sought. The crop factor also effectively extends telephoto lenses. A 300mm lens on an APS-C camera equals 450mm (or 480mm on Canon; Canon just has to be bloody different!)

The reason this is important is because you need to consider the crop factor when you are deciding which focal length prime lens will work best for you.

And that's really the key to the whole issue of how to choose a prime lens.

For example, I thought I would prefer a 35mm

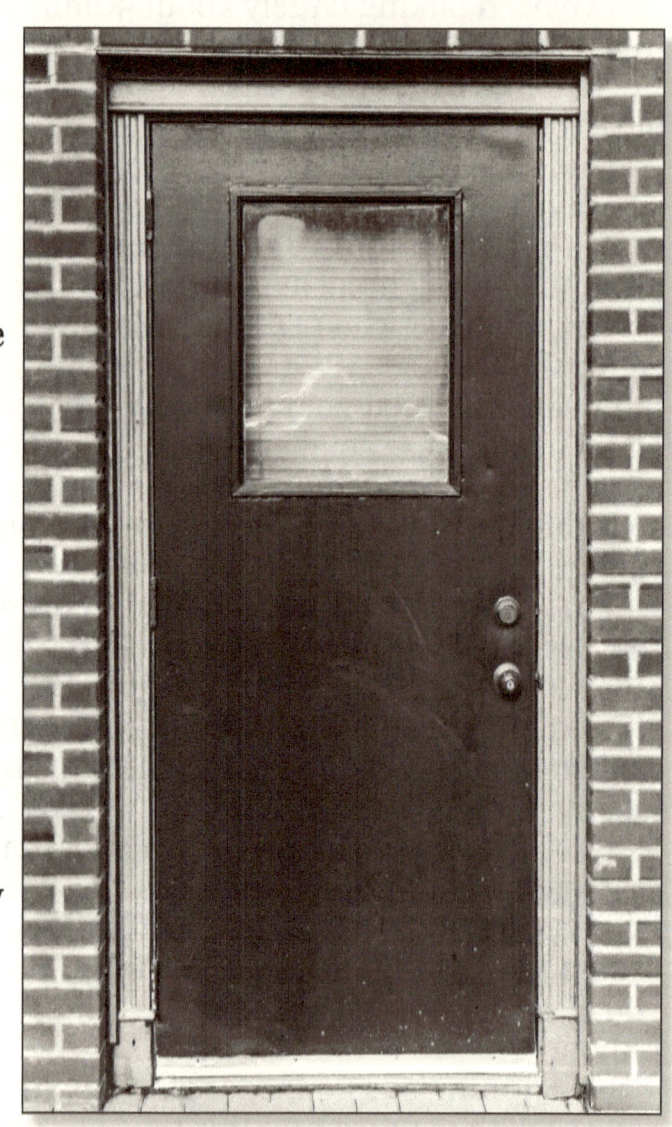

Saratoga Springs, N.Y., Nov. 22, 2014.
Nikon D7000, 28mm (prime), 1/2000, f/2.8, ISO 250, S, spot metering.
© 2014, 2015 by Shawn M. Tomlinson

lens for my Nikon D7000 and other Nikon DSLRs because it is the APS-C camera equivalent of a "normal" lens (35 x 1.5 = 52.5).

The D7000 crop factor takes 35mm to 52.5mm. So, when I had the opportunity to test a Nikon G 35mm f/1.8 lens, I was thrilled.

Then I had the opportunity to test an older model Nikon AF D 28mm (28 x 1.5 = 42) which is just a slight wide-angle and I found the prime lens for me for the APS-C cameras. For the full-frame Nikon D800e, the 50mm works perfectly for me.

You may want a slightly wider or slightly longer prime lens for your own use because each lens gives you a different perspective. One may fit your uses and vision better than another.

The main focal lengths for prime lenses listed here

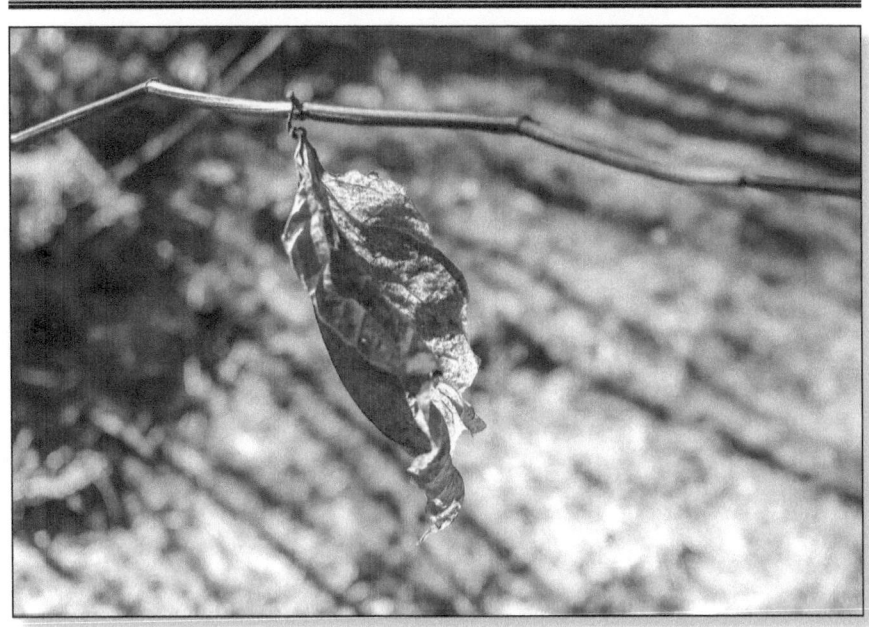

Indian Kill Nature Preserve, Glenville, N.Y., Nov. 15, 2014.
Nikon D7000, 28mm (prime), 1/800, f/4, ISO 320, S, pattern metering.
© 2014, 2015 by Shawn M. Tomlinson

include the actual focal length on 1.5x and 1.6x DSLRs with the respective angles of view for 1.5x cameras:

10mm (15mm; 16mm)	=	angle of view: 109° 20'
12mm (18mm; 19.2mm)	=	angle of view: 99° 10'
14mm (21mm; 22.4mm)	=	angle of view: 90° 20'
16mm (24mm; 25.6mm)	=	angle of view: 82° 50'
18mm (27mm; 28.8mm)	=	angle of view: 76° 10'
20mm (30mm; 32mm)	=	angle of view: 70° 20'
24mm (36mm; 38.4mm)	=	angle of view: 60° 50'
28mm (42mm; 44.8mm)	=	angle of view: 53° 30'
35mm (52.5mm; 56mm)	=	angle of view: 43° 50'
50mm (75mm; 80mm)	=	angle of view: 31° 30'
85mm (127.5mm; 136mm)	=	angle of view: 18° 50'
100mm (150mm; 160mm)	=	angle of view: 16° 00'
105mm (157.5mm; 168mm)	=	angle of view: 15° 20'
200mm (300mm; 320mm)	=	angle of view: 8° 00'
300mm (450mm; 480mm)	=	angle of view: 5° 20'

Some of these are based largely upon what film photographers used for decades and still like to use.

The 24mm lens once was just about the widest-angle lens you could get before the rounding fisheye effect crept in. Advances in technology have broken this limit, but the 24mm remains as a significant lens in most lineups.

On a full-frame or film camera, it gives an angle of view of 83° 60'. On an APS-C DSLR it's 60° 50'.

The 24mm lens usual has a maximum aperture of f/1.4 or f/1.8, making it a very bright lens, very usable in low-light conditions.

The 28mm lens (42mm; 44.8mm) was, as I mentioned the widest standard prime for many years in film photography. I personally like this focal length for a prime, but you may not, especially if you want a lot of bokeh. I can get bokeh with it, but the wider the angle of view of a lens, the more that is in focus and the less bokeh you get. I get some by moving in as close as I can to the subject, but a 50mm (75mm; 80mm) or 85mm (127.5mm; 136mm) is better for better bokeh.

The thing I like best about the 28mm is that it has that hint of wide-angle-ness to it, but also doesn't push everything so far away it is difficult to see.

On a full-frame or film camera, it gives an angle of view of 75° 20'. On an APS-C DSLR it's 53° 30'.

Next up is the 35mm

Wolfarth's Pond Park, Gloversville, N.Y., Nov. 21, 2014.
Nikon D7000, 28mm (prime), 1/8000, f/3.2, ISO 400, S, spot metering.
© 2014, 2015 by Shawn M. Tomlinson

prime. This used to be the poor man's wide-angle lens. It wasn't that wide, but a little, and that made it cheaper than the 28mm and much cheaper than the 24mm. It isn't used much on full-frame cameras, but on APS-C DSLRs, it serves as a perfect standard view lens.

On a full-frame camera, it gives an angle of view of 63° 20'. On an APS-C DSLR it's 43° 50'.

I'm very glad the 50mm lens still exists because although it does not serve the same purpose it once did for APS-C DSLRs, it still has a great purpose.

Because of its apparent increase in focal length (75mm; 80mm) and its short focal plane at wide-open aperture, it can isolate a subject — such as a person — from the background wonderfully. The bokeh effect can be stunning. And because 50mm lenses can have very bright maximum apertures — f/1.8, f/1.4 and f/1.2 — they are fantastic for natural light and indoor photography.

On a full-frame or film camera, it gives an angle of view of 46° 40'. On an APS-C DSLR it's 31° 30'.

Finally, the 85mm (127.5mm; 136mm) lens. These, as short telephotos, make even better portrait lenses than 50mm lenses, and give even better bokeh. These also have very bright maximum apertures, the same as a 50mm: f/1.8, f/1.4 and f/1.2. These and the 24mm lenses typically have the better build qualities than the 28mm, 35mm or 50mm, but that costs a premium.

Canon makes two 100mm macro lenses. At the top is the Canon EF L 100mm f/2.8 macro with the non-L Canon EF 100mm f/2.8 USM macro at about half the price.

My new favorite, though, is the 105mm from Nikon that has both vibration reduction (VR) and macro capabilities. It can serve as both a good portrait lens with lots of bokeh or a short telephoto or as a 1:1 macro lens. Nikon's version (the one I use) has a maximum aperture of f/2.8, which is pretty standard for a good macro lens. Nikon calls "macro" "micro" in case you are looking for such a lens.

I had been shooting with a Nikon AF D 28mm f/2.8 and a Nikon AF D 50mm f/1.8 and even a Nikon G 35mm f/1.8 lenses a lot before I acquired the 105mm f/2.8, but I fell in love with this incredible lens. Certainly, I will shoot with the aforementioned shorter focal-length lenses again, but the quality of Nikon's 105mm just astounds me.

The moment I put it on the Nikon D800e, there was an obvious difference. This is a classic case that proves the constant advice that good glass is essential to good photographs.

Admittedly, the D800e and 105mm combination costs — even used — significantly more than most cameras and lenses I recommend, and certainly you do not need the best camera and best lens to take magnificent photographs.

However, as you develop your photographic skills, you will want better lenses and better cameras. You will notice differences that the casual observer will not.

For example, my stepgranddaughter and I were out shooting the other day. She's 10 and learning about photography. She has a natural instinct for it that is quite interesting. Certainly not every photo she takes is fantastic, but on nearly every voyage of photography upon which we have embarked, she gets at least a few really good shots. And her percentage increases the more we go.

So, I handed her my Canon EOS 20D with the

Canon EF II 50mm f/1.8 lens and I was carrying the Nikon D800e and Nikon AF-S 105mm f/2.8 lens. We shot many of the same subjects, so when I started looking at the photos to process them, my first instinct was that something had gone wrong with the 20D. I noticed a lack of detail in the background of her photos.

Then I realized that it was because already my eye had become accustom to the D800e and 105mm lens.

There was nothing wrong with the Canon EOS 20D and the Canon EF II 50mm f/1.8 was as sharp as ever. She took some great photos.

You will notice many photos in this book from the Nikon AF-S 105mm f/2.8 lens. This is a change from the eBook version because I simply did not have access to this lens when I wrote this originally. I also did not have access to some of the other primes I have since shot with, so I am including a wider variety of photos from these different primes in this expanded book.

The more I learn as a I shoot every day, the more I understand about what each lens can do. This will happen to you, as well.

As a photographer, for example, I now realize the importance of prime lenses, although I also realize not every photographer is having the same love affair with them that I am. Zoom lenses still are useful and important in many circumstances.

Yet, give me a prime over a zoom in nearly any circumstance and I'll be happier.

No matter how good the zoom lens is, in nearly every circumstance, a good prime lens will beat it. It will give me the detail I crave, even if nobody else notices the difference.

Nikon's 105mm is the best lens I've ever shot with.

Canon's 100mm macro lens compares quite favorably. This focal length may not suit your shooting style and subjects, though, so consider that when considering a prime lens.

There certainly are other prime lenses at different focal lengths, but these are the most commonly used. Others include ultra-wide-angle lenses such as a 14mm or 15mm, and telephotos such as 200mm, 300mm, 400mm, etc. The 20mm lens also has possibilities.

The ironic thing about this is that most of us who started in the film SLR days likely first shot with prime lenses. From 1959 until at least the 1980s, the prime lens was the standard for most beginners and pros.

The reason for this was that zoom lenses — then made of metal, not the plastic common in many zooms today — were heavy and the optics weren't that good. They also — then and now — had smaller maximum apertures than primes, which meant slower shutter speeds, which meant more likelihood of lens blur from camera shake.

Somehow, though, as the optics got better and camera makers started using plastic instead of metal as a primary material, the zoom lens replaced the prime as the typical lens sold with or just after the purchase of a single-lens reflex camera.

Zooms — again, then and now — appeal more to beginners and amateurs because, like Yoda said about the Dark Side, they are quicker and easier than primes. Those new to DSLR photography see the versatility of zooms as more important than the quality of primes. They also can get zoom lenses much cheaper than primes.

I fell into this trap myself way back when. As a new

photographer and teenager, I believed I was severely limited by my "crappy old" 50mm lens. I did not realize how good that smc Pentax 50mm f/1.8 manual lens was until many years later when I put it on my Pentax K20D DSLR and started shooting.

I was so blown away by the quality, I new prime lenses were in my future.

But, back in the 1970s and 1980s, I yearned for zoom lenses. As soon as they got cheap enough, I bought a couple. Once the autofocus era began, zoom lenses became "kit" lenses making them the main — and often only — lenses for beginners. This carried over into the digital photography age, and continues now.

Perhaps other than acquiring a better DSLR, moving to a really good prime lens is the best sign that you are become serious about your photography.

PART 3: APERTURE

I've mentioned a lot about aperture, but what exactly do these numbers mean?

Think about it this way.

An aperture of f/1 would mean the lens "sees" the same amount of light that your eyes do.

As the number increases from f/1, a lens gets darker or "slower," meaning it lets in less light.

So, a lens with a maximum aperture of f/1.2 would allow you to shoot in less light than one with a maximum aperture of f/1.8.

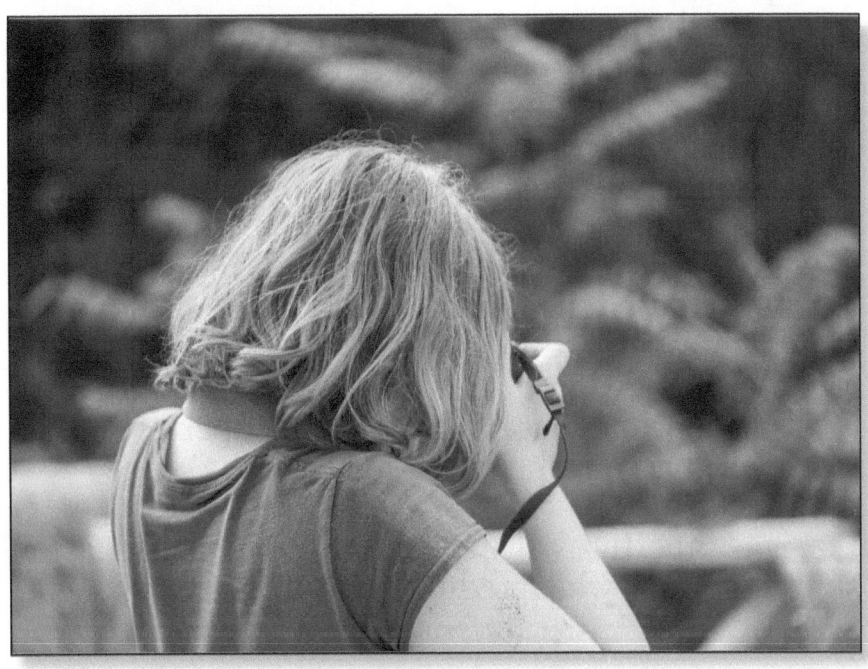

Kara, Ballston Lake, NY, July 10, 2015
Nikon D800e, 105mm, 1/200, f/3.5, ISO 400, S, pattern metering
© 2015 by Shawn M. Tomlinson

All of the prime lenses listed here have brighter maximum apertures than average zoom lenses.

Standard 18-55mm "kit" lenses for APS-C DSLRs typically have maximum apertures of $f/3.5$, but that gets darker as you zoom, usually down to $f/5.6$ or $f/6.3$.

A better zoom will give you a single maximum aperture, usually $f/2.8$ or $f/4$, at all focal lengths. And, it should be noted that Sigma has been introducing really good zoom lens with constant apertures that are brighter than previously possible. The trade off is that these lenses have shorter zoom ranges. For example, the Sigma 18-35mm $f/1.8$ DC HSM. No one had produced such a lens previously with as bright a maximum aperture. I have not tried one, but my guess is that, as a zoom, as good as it may be, this lens will not give quite the results of a prime.

One of the best things about using a prime lens — apart from the sharpness and reduced or eliminated chromatic aberrations and distortion — is your new-found ability to shoot without a flash in situations you never would have dreamed of with your zoom lens.

For example, unless you push the ISO sensitivity of your DSLR way up to the stupid ISOs — above 800 — you usually cannot shoot a night scene of a lone streetlight with your $f/3.5$ zoom.

At least not without a long exposure and a tripod.

Using a prime that has a maximum aperture of $f/1.2$ will give you a beautiful image of the scene hand-held.

Bigger apertures also mean the ability to use faster shutter speeds, which reduces blur from lens shake.

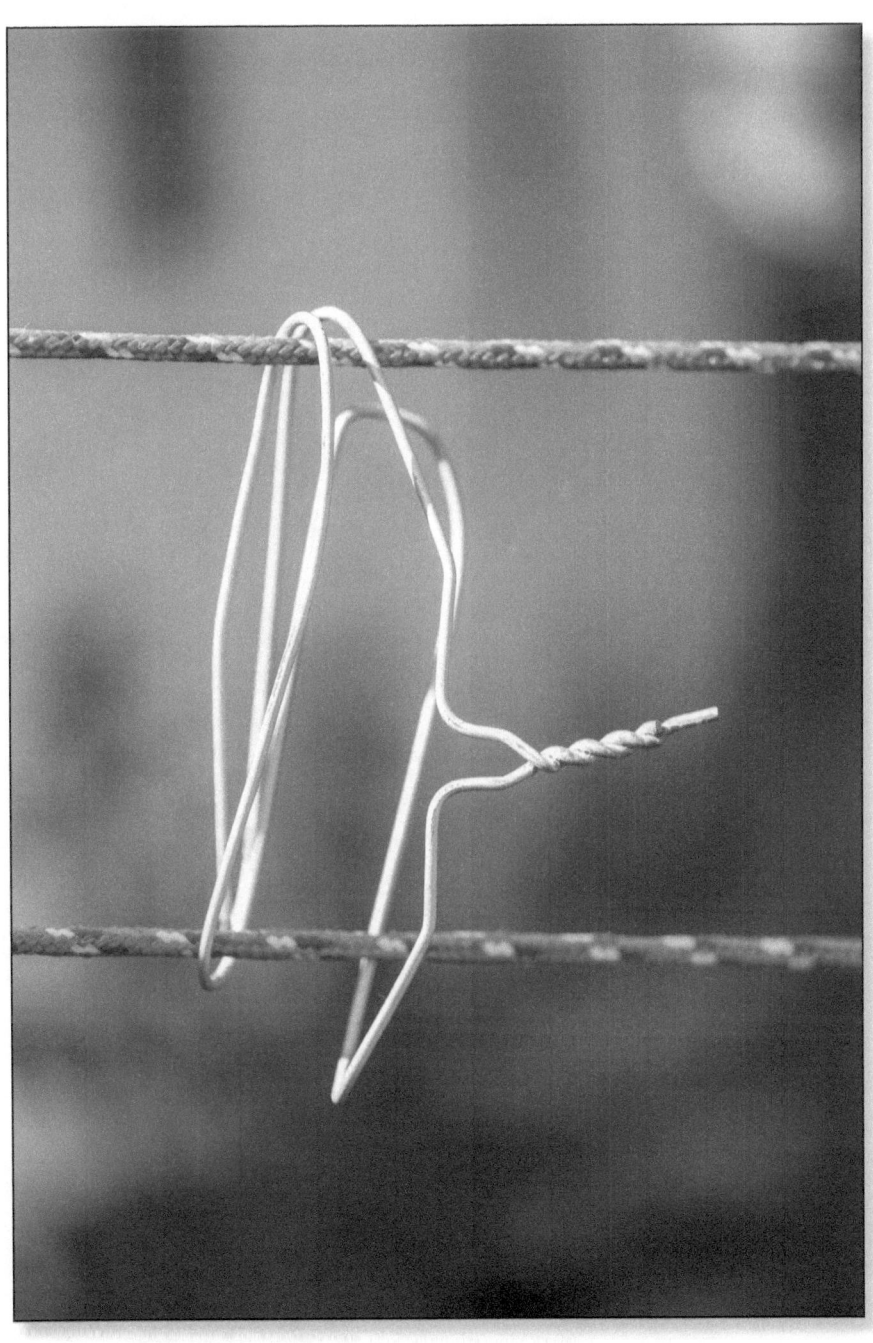

Ballston Lake, NY, July 11, 2015
Nikon D800e, 105mm, 1/1000, f/3, ISO 200, S, pattern metering
© 2015 by Shawn M. Tomlinson

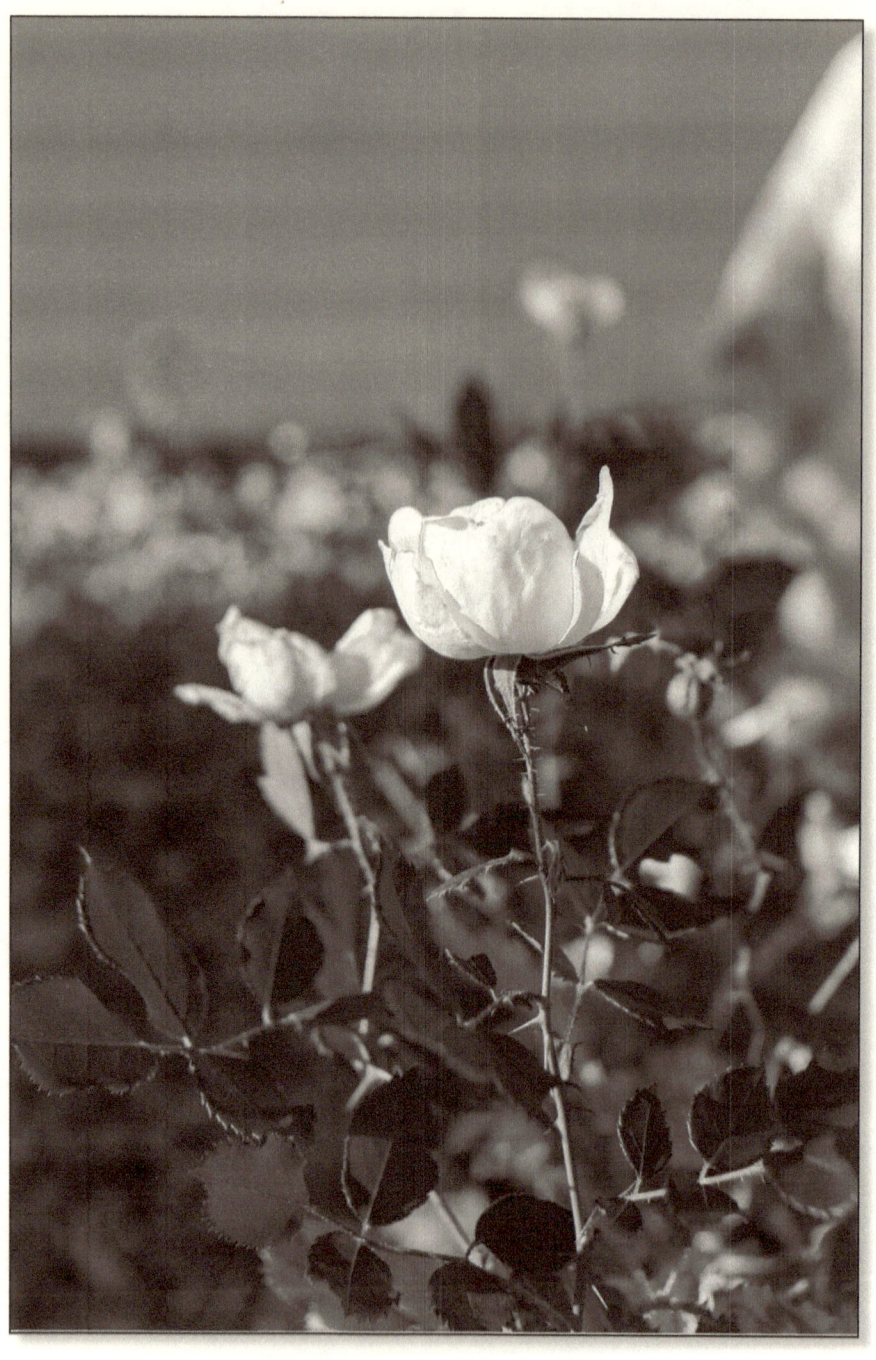

Ballston Lake, N.Y., Nov. 12, 2014.
Nikon D7000, 28mm (prime), 1/500, f/3.5, ISO 100, S, spot metering.
© 2014 by Shawn M. Tomlinson

PART 4: PRICES

Several things dictate the prices of prime lenses:
• Glass quality
• Build quality
• Maximum aperture

To give you an idea of prices differences based upon these three factors, here are Canon and Nikon prices for 50mm primes lenses as of this writing:

Lens Name	Maximum Aperture	List Price
Canon EF L 50mm	f/1.2	$1,550
Canon EF 50mm	f/1.4	$400
Canon EF II 50mm	f/1.8	$126
AF Nikkor 50mm	f/1.2	$725
AF-S Nikkor G 50mm	f/1.4	$470
AF D Nikkor 50mm	f/1.8	$135

Canon designates its best lenses with "L" and they have a red ring near the front of the barrels. It should be noted that since the first edition of this book, Canon has replaced its venerable and excellent EF II 50mm f/1.8 lens with the EF STM 50mm f/1.8 for about the same price. Apart from newer technology, the replacement also has a metal lens mount, making it a sturdier, stronger lens.

The main reason for the price disparity between the f/1.2 Nikon and Canon lenses is that Canon's is the newest, latest technology, while Nikon's is a left-over from the early days of autofocus lenses, although the company still lists it as manufactured and for sale.

It still has top-quality glass, but does not have

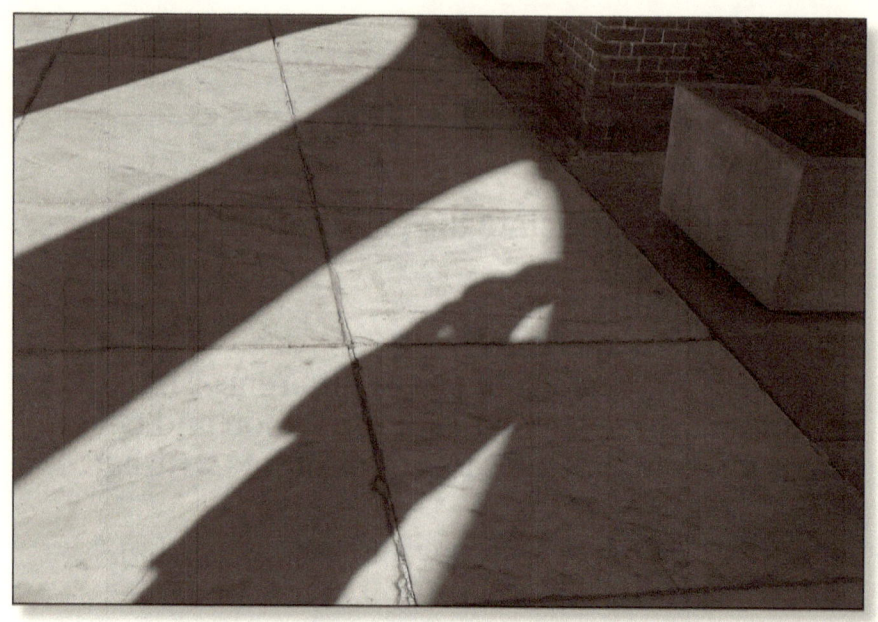

Gary W. Ziroli, Roosevelt Baths, Saratoga Springs, N.Y., Nov. 11, 2014.
Nikon D7000, 28mm (prime), 1/320, f/10, ISO 200, S, pattern metering.
© 2014, 2015 by Shawn M. Tomlinson

some of the latest features. For example, without the "AF D" or "AF-S" designation, later Nikon DSLRs cannot auto correct distortion and chromatic aberration in-camera. None of Canon's DSLRs offer this kind of auto correction except the top pro EOS 1DX. All of Nikon's DSLRs after 2008 have this feature, but only with Nikon AF-D and later lenses, and not those made by third-parties such as Sigma, Tamron and Tokina.

Not to despair, though from this price list. Used photographic equipment can be just as good as new as long as you purchase from reputable dealers. Buying from eBay or the guy in the alley is a crap shoot: you may get a great lens or you may not.

There probably are others, but the only U.S.-based

reputable dealer in used (and new) photographic equipment is KEH.com. I prefer KEH because on the rare occasions I have gotten equipment that does not work properly, KEH has been the best company I've ever worked with. Others have been nightmares, especially the two big ones in NYC.

Case in point: I bought a Nikon D70 — very low-end, very old, very cheap at $79 — in January 2014. It had continual dust problems on the sensor which I needed to clean every day before shooting, and it had difficulties with memory cards. Sometimes it would read CF cards, sometimes it wouldn't. Sometimes it didn't record images at all, but left empty files.

It did these things from the beginning but I worked around them. They kept getting worse. In late July, I contacted KEH, told them the problems and

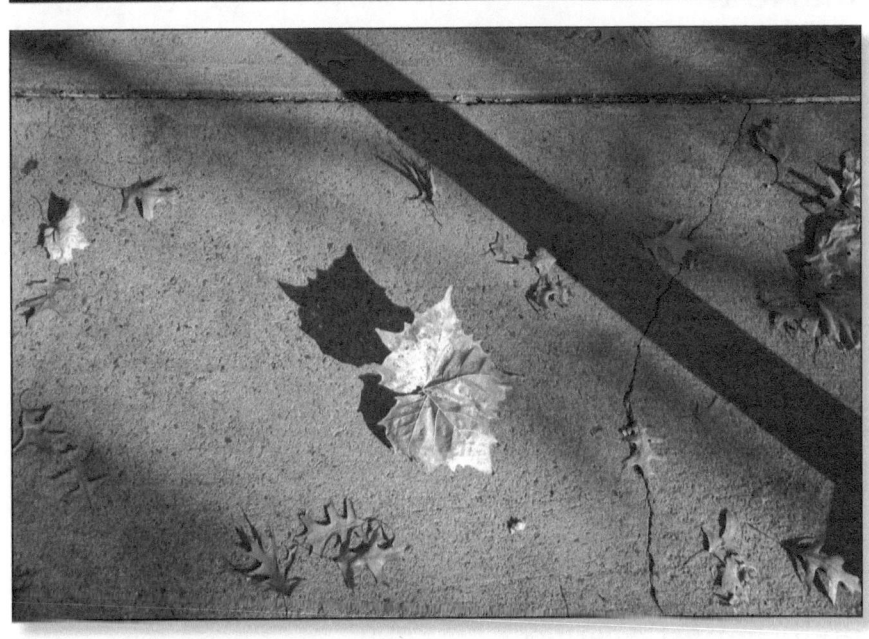

Roosevelt Baths, Saratoga Springs, N.Y., Nov. 11, 2014.
Nikon D7000, 28mm (prime), 1/400, f/8, ISO 200, S, pattern metering.
© 2014, 2015 by Shawn M. Tomlinson

immediately they sent me the information to return it and paid for return shipping. A few days later, I got a D70 that worked properly and still does. All this for $79.

I'm sticking with KEH.

I have had only bad experiences with Adorama and B&H. Their prices usually are a little higher than KEH, too. I started with KEH

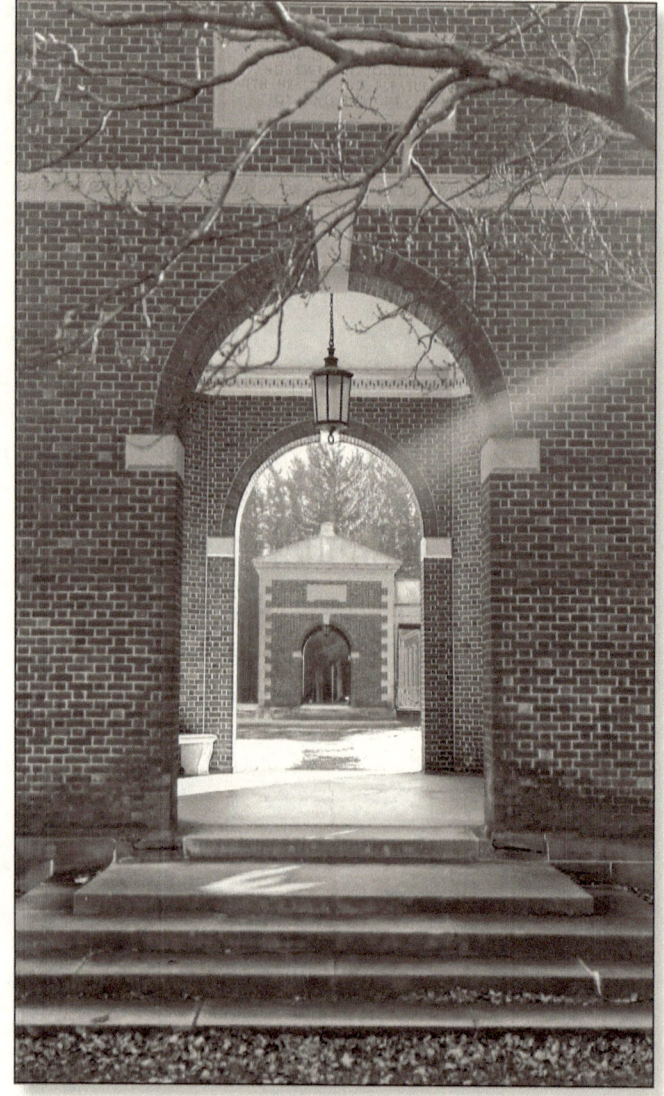

Roosevelt Baths, Saratoga Springs, N.Y., Nov. 11, 2014.
Nikon D7000, 28mm (prime), 1/1000, f/2.8, ISO 200, S, pattern metering.
© 2014, 2015 by Shawn M. Tomlinson

because of a sports photographer's recommendation, and I will stick with this company as long as it keeps up its fantastic service.

Apart from all this great customer service, KEH

has a strict grading system for lenses and cameras. Its prices are dictated by the over all grade KEH gives the piece of equipment. So, for example, KEH lists a Sigma 18-50mm macro lens at the BGN (bargain) rating for $218. The same lens in LN- (like new minus) condition has a price of $328.

The key to buying a good lens used is being able to trust the grading system of the seller. This is where eBay — with its many and varied sellers — cannot compete. Each seller may rate differently, so "Excellent" to a seller might appear "Bargain" to you.

Again, I am extolling the virtues of KEH — and no, the company does not pay me or compensate me in anyway; probably other than the orders I place with them, does not even know I exist — but I must say that virtually everything I've ever bought from the company graded as BGN I would grade much higher. And for a little bit — or a lot — more money, EX, EX+ and LN- rated equipment is even better from KEH.

What all this means is that you can get your prime lens new in the box from Canon, Nikon, Pentax or Sony with the nifty instructions and all — and if price isn't a problem, do it — or you can get the same lens cheaper used.

One more advantage in some cases of buying older used lenses is that they often still have aperture rings on them. The camera makers, to cut costs, have eliminated aperture rings on many lenses. The camera body controls the aperture or you can do it manually using the DSLR's command dials, but there's nothing quite like the solid feel of a lens with an aperture ring. So, for example, none of Nikon's lenses designated as "G" have aperture rings, but the older "AF" and "AF D" lenses do. You may not need the aperture ring, but I find it useful.

So let's look at those same lenses listed above for Nikon and Canon to see what you can get them for (at the time of this writing) previously used. I have listed KEH's grading mark in (EX) after the price. KEH grades go from the low UG (ugly) to BGN (bargain), EX (Excellent), EX+ (excellent-plus), LN- (like new but without the box and accessories) and LN (like new with all the accessories that came with it originally).

Both of the f/1.2 lenses are a little harder to find on the used market, probably because the companies make fewer of them. Pros like f/1.2 lenses, but the prices often put off amateurs and semi-pros, so the initial retail market is smaller.

Lens Name	Max Aperture	List Price	Used Price
Canon EF L 50mm	f/1.2	$1,550	$1,119 (EX)
Canon EF 50mm	f/1.4	$400	$278 (EX)
Canon EF 50mm	f/1.8	$126	$79 (BGN)
AF Nikkor 50mm	f/1.2	$725	$448 (EX)
AF-S Nikkor G 50mm	f/1.4	$470	$248 (EX)
AF D Nikkor 50mm	f/1.8	$135	$99 (EX)

Prices for other primes usually are higher simply because the original manufacturers' price is higher.

No matter who tells you price doesn't matter and you should just spend the money to get the best lens possible, we all know price *does* matter to most of us. So the compromise is: what is cost-effective and what do you need?

Sure, it would be great to have a 50mm f/1.2 prime, but is the extra cost worth it? So, with the 50mm lens, it really comes down to a choice between the f/1.4 and the f/1.8.

Since the optics are about the same between these two, the main difference you are paying for — other than that two-thirds of an f-stop difference, which isn't much — is the build quality. Because pros more than enthusiasts or amateurs buy the f/1.4 lens, it is built better. It has more metal then plastic, handles well and smoothly, etc. This means the f/1.4 typically costs three times as much.

Build quality certainly is important, but

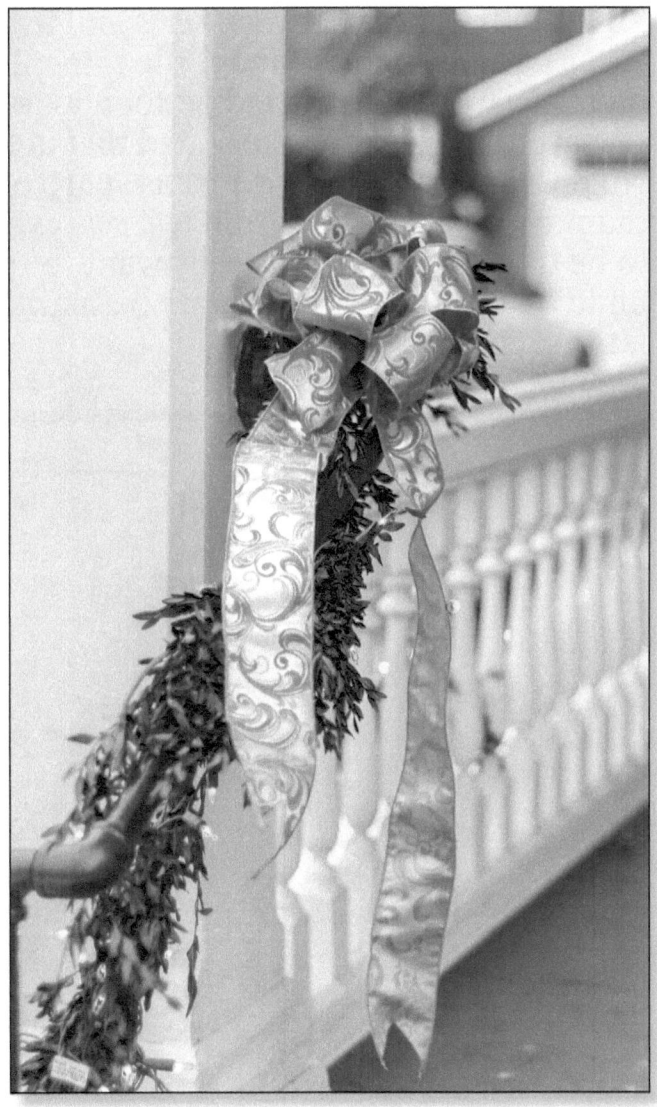

Saratoga Springs, N.Y., Dec. 16, 2014.
Nikon D70, 50mm (prime), 1/200, f/2.5, ISO 400, S, spot metering.
© 2014, 2015 by Shawn M. Tomlinson

if you are not banging your DSLR and lenses around constantly, daily on the job as a pro photographer — and if you are cautious — the plastic 50mm lenses will serve you well.

The differences between f/1.4 and f/1.8 lenses in other focal lengths are about the same. The f/1.4 almost always is constructed better and is sturdier.

Several reviewers have stated that at least for Nikon, the f/1.8 50mm is just as sharp or sharper than the f/1.4 version. From test scores, this appears to be true, so unless you really want the superior build quality, optically, you are better off with the f/1.8 version.

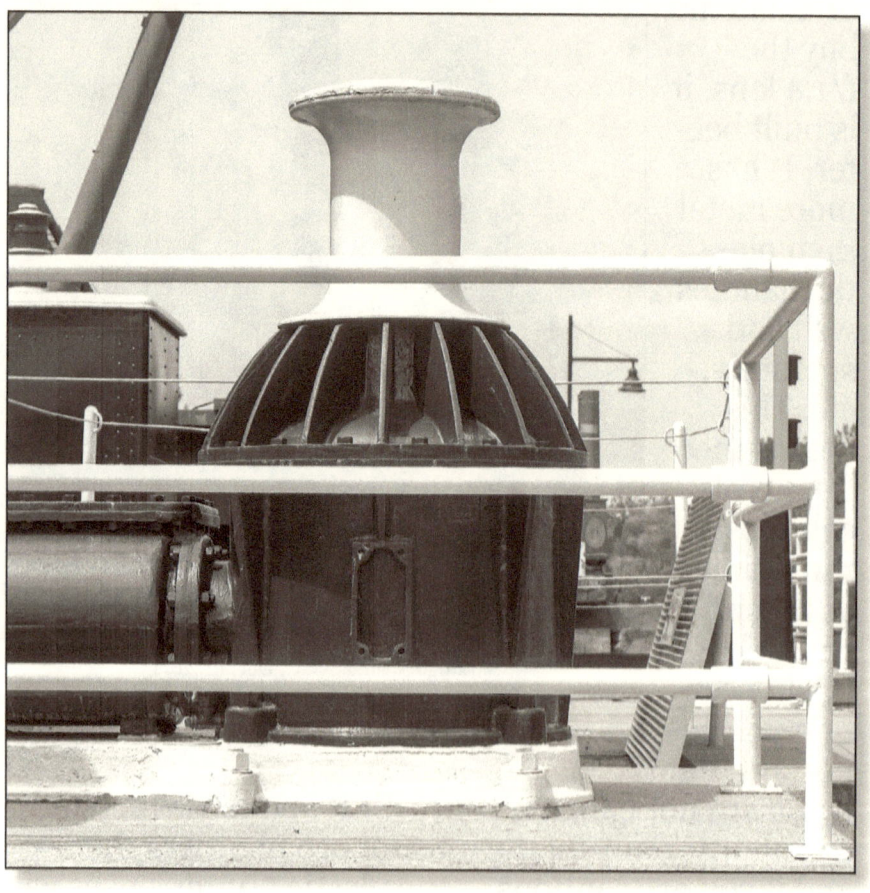

Lock C-5, Schuylerville, NY, May 16, 2015
Nikon D2x 50mm, 1/500, f/9, ISO 250, S, pattern metering
© 2015 by Shawn M. Tomlinson

It just depends if that is worth paying significantly more for.

If you have an actual, physical camera store you can get to in person, do it. They are becoming rare outside of big cities, at least in the United States. If you can get to such a store, that is the best way to test and determine which focal length prime will suit your shooting style best.

The key is to take your own DSLR and your own memory card to the store. Shoot a few photos in the store with each lens, but also ask the clerk to step outside with you so you can shoot some tests in an environment more akin to where you will be shooting with the lens once you own it. Shoot the same scenes with different focal length lenses.

Take the memory card home, open the photos in your photo editing software and examine them, certainly for sharpness, chromatic aberration, etc., but mainly for which focal length you like best.

If you do not have a nearby camera store, you can rent lenses online, or you can try a lens simulator. There are several available free online. I like Nikon's simulator, of course, but their are others. These allow you to look at the same scene with virtually any focal length lens. It's not quite as good as testing each lens in the field, but it will give you a good idea of which focal length lens you like best.

The easiest way, though, to test the different focal lengths is using your own zoom. An 18-55mm lens covers several of these focal lengths, so set your zoom to 28mm, for example, and shoot some test shots. Try it with the other focal lengths, too.

Just remember not to touch that zoom ring, and shoot consistently with the same focal length for a given set of images.

So, for example, go to a nearby park and shoot 10 images at 24mm, then 10 at 28mm, etc. It is useful to be able to compare the focal lengths using the exact same scene, so use a tripod if you have one.

Do the same comparison on your computer display to determine which focal-length lens you like best.

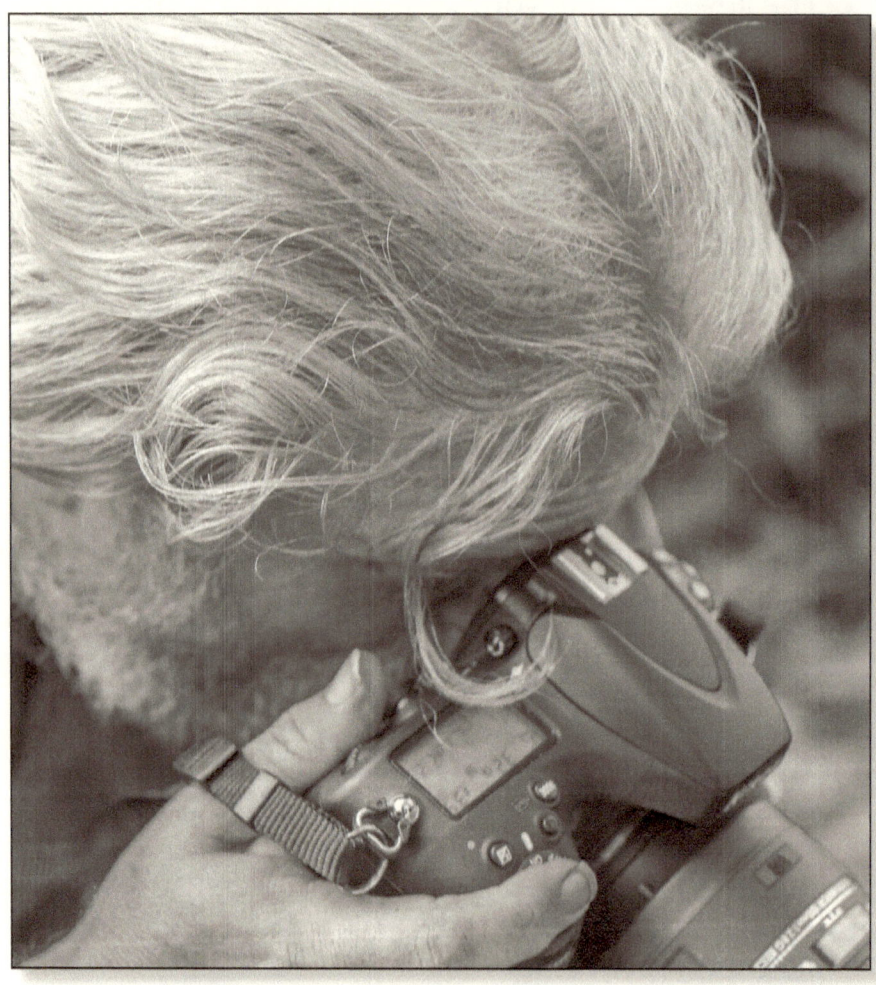

Shawn Tomlinson, Ballston Lake, NY, July 10, 2015
Canon EOS 20D, 50mm, 1/125, f/3.2, ISO 400, P, pattern metering
Photo by Kara Kutny © 2015 by Shawn M. Tomlinson

PART 5: AND IN THE END...

You probably don't need more than one, two tops, of these prime lenses unless you are a pro and need them for very specific uses.

My recommendation is to get one wide-angle and one slight telephoto prime lens if you want two. I had a 28mm and traded it for a 50mm. I do want to add a wide-angle zoom — either a 20mm or 24mm — as soon as I can, but these pretty much will be all I need outside of a 300mm or 400mm prime lens down the road.

The reason I traded the 28mm for the 50mm is that I know that because I like the 50mm focal length, I will use it more. I will add a wide-angle prime for those other times that the 50mm has too narrow an angle of view.

In most cases, the most useful prime lenses for the most photographers are the 28mm or 35mm for APS-C cameras. They give you the most versatility and work well as complements to your zoom lenses.

If, for example, you use a travel lens, an 18-200mm super zoom, you have most of the focal lengths covered. These lenses give a range of 27-300mm in full-frame terms. Not super wide, but certainly super long. To make these lenses so versatile, manufacturers typically must compromise the optical quality at some focal lengths, usually at either end. They are getting better and they are useful.

And, yes, they can be set at 28mm or 35mm, but the clarity and sharpness will not be as good as either of these focal lengths in prime lenses. You also won't get the kind of maximum aperture with a travel lens

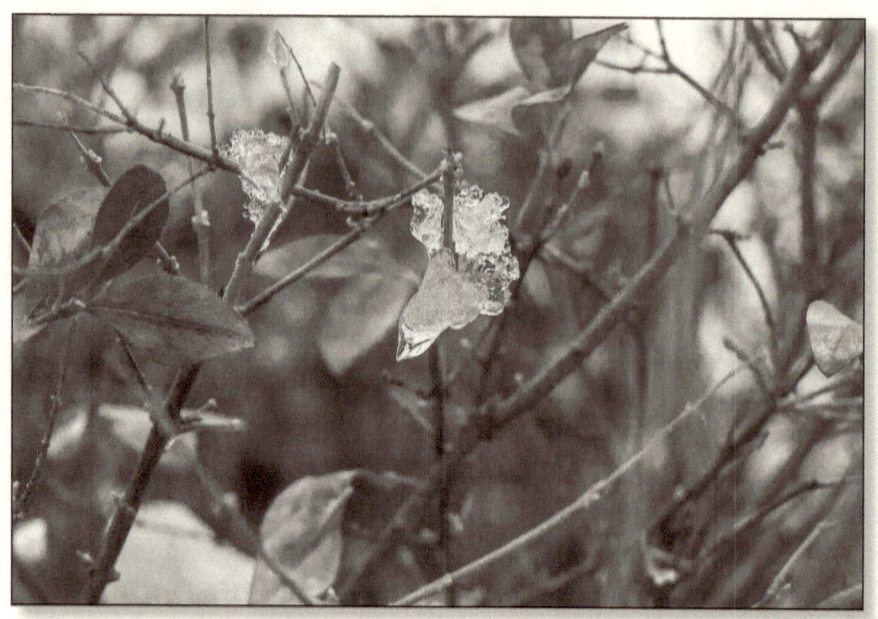

Saratoga Springs, N.Y., Dec. 16, 2014.
Nikon D70, 50mm (prime), 1/200, f/5, ISO 400, S, spot metering.
© 2014, 2015 by Shawn M. Tomlinson

that you will with a prime.

So, even though an 18-200mm travel lens, or even an 18-55mm kit lens will cover the same focal length as one of these prime lenses, the primes will give you advantages over the zooms. For this reason, adding a prime lens to your photographic arsenal is a good idea.

Once you graduate beyond the travel lens — and most of us do, except for, well, traveling (the reason they're called travel lenses is because they allow you to get all the focal lengths without needing to carry multiple lenses. This lightens your load and makes for quicker shooting) — your lens lineup should look something like this:

- 10-20mm ultra-wide zoom (or 12-24mm)
- 24-105mm (Canon) or 24-120mm (Nikon)

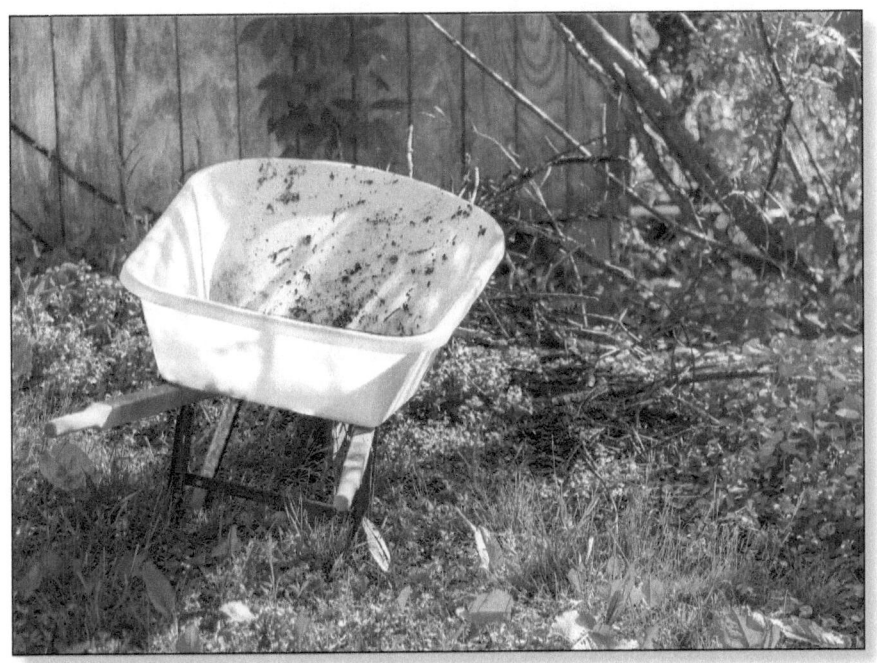

Ballston Lake, NY, May 22, 2015
Nikon D7000, 50mm, 1/1000, f/2.8, ISO 200, S, pattern metering
© 2015 by Shawn M. Tomlinson

- 28mm or 35mm prime
- 70-300mm
- 300mm prime

You may have variations within this proposed lineup, but these five lenses will give you virtually every normal photographic possibility. Together on an APS-C DSLR, they give you an effective focal length range of 15mm to 450mm for Nikon, Pentax and Sony, or 16mm to 480mm for Canon.

The reason I include two primes — the 28mm or 35mm and the 300mm — is that these have very specific uses. The 28mm or 35mm give you normal focal length, while the 300mm is useful for extreme bokeh and shooting from far away when your subjects are such things as wildlife or public events. You can't really get that close to the subjects in these situations, so a good prime 300mm will give you the reach you need.

The other use for a 300mm — or 400mm or on up if you have the money; Canon's 800mm telephoto prime has a list price of $13,500 and Nikon's 800mm goes for $17,900 — the one to which I intend to put mine most often, is photographing near subjects very close. Using my 70-300mm at the 300mm end has proven to me just how fantastic images of such subjects as simple as flowers can be.

Oh, sure, I'll probably use the 300mm prime for distance sometimes, but my fascination with the extreme detail and bokeh possibilities probably won't end soon.

The only reason I have not covered longer primes or shorter primes as much in this book is that they are expensive, out of the reach of most non-pros and are, in general, less universally useful than those I've, ahem, focused upon.

What it comes down to is that prime lenses almost always are superior to zooms in sharpness, lack of distortion and eliminating or at least minimizing chromatic aberrations.

If I need to shoot fast at varying distances, yes, I'll still use a zoom lens.

If I can just take a tiny bit more time, I always use my prime lens for better results.

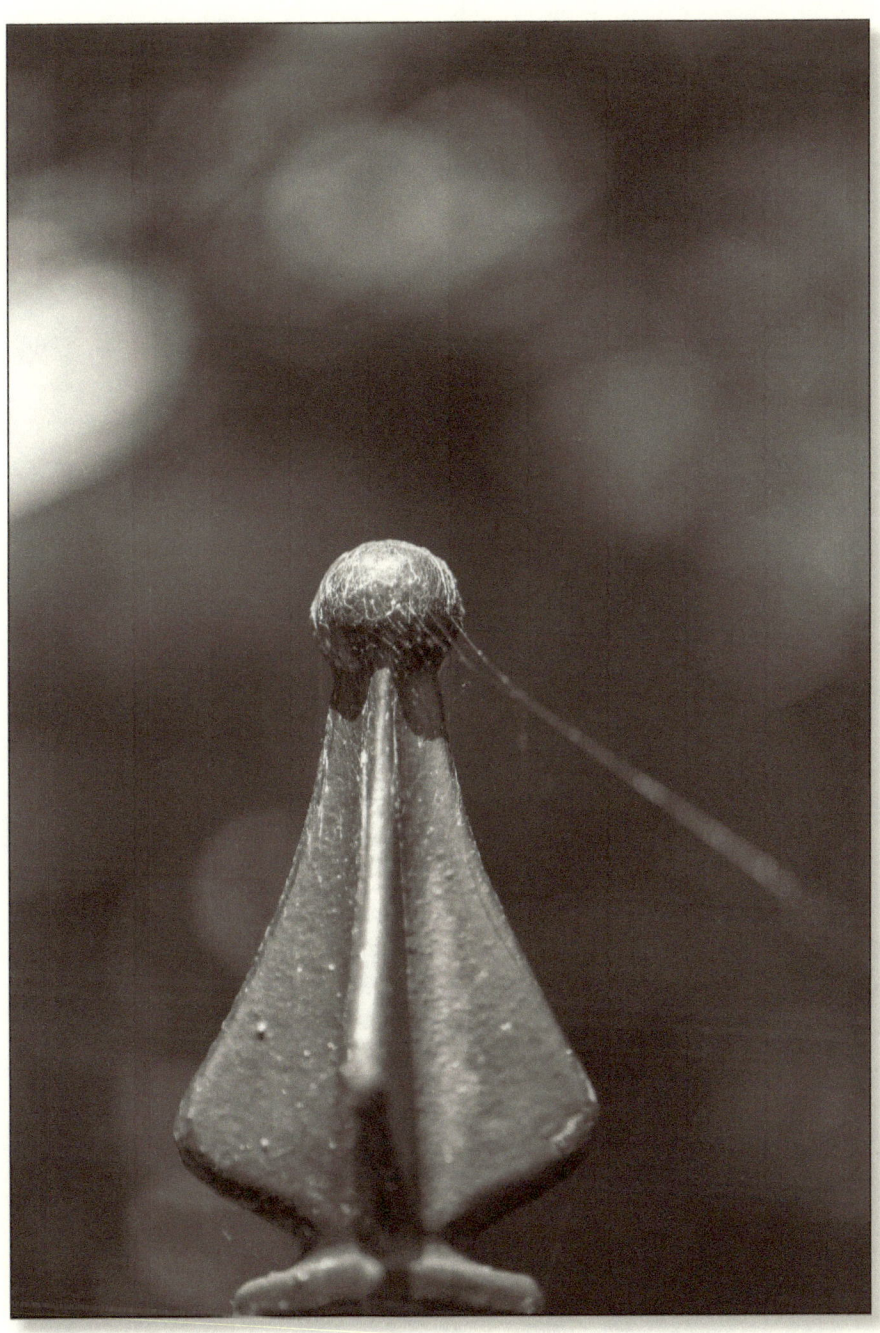

Saratoga Springs, NY, July 11, 2015
Nikon D800e, 105mm, 1/1000, f/3, ISO 200, S, pattern metering
© 2015 by Shawn M. Tomlinson

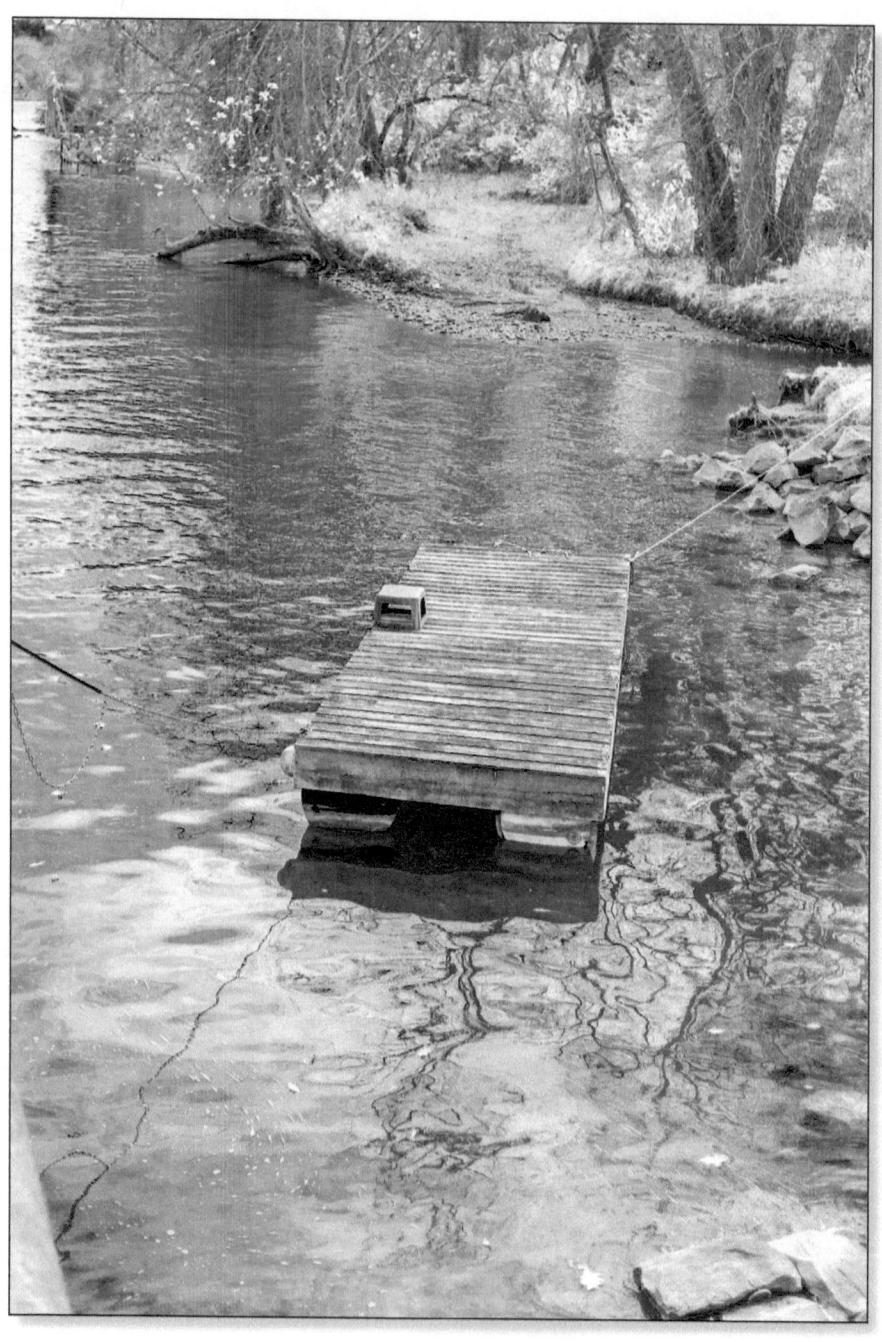

Schuylerville, N.Y., Nov. 8, 2014.
Nikon D7000, 35mm (prime), 1/3200, f/2, ISO 250, S, pattern metering.
© 2014 by Shawn M. Tomlinson

Shawn M. Tomlinson's Guide to Photography Series

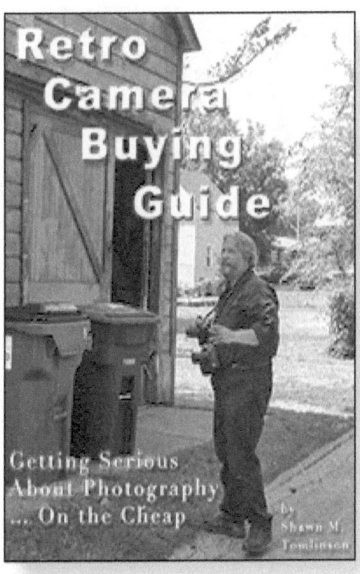

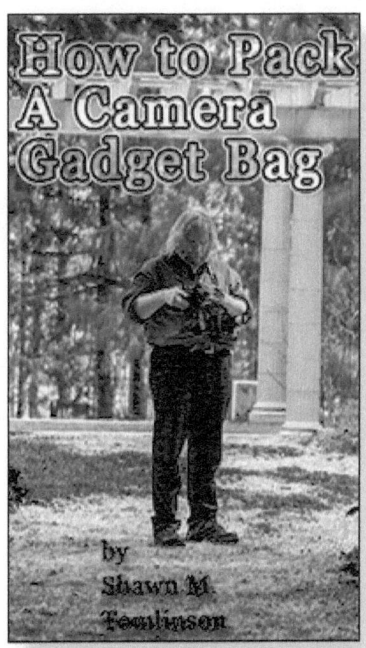

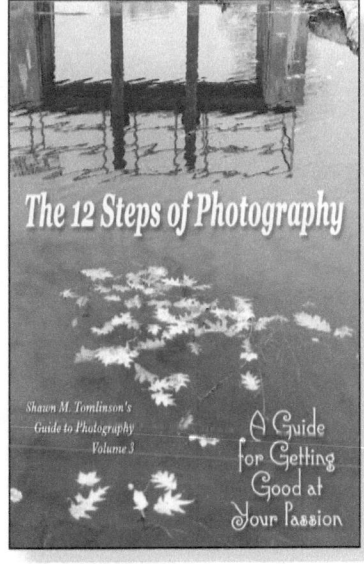

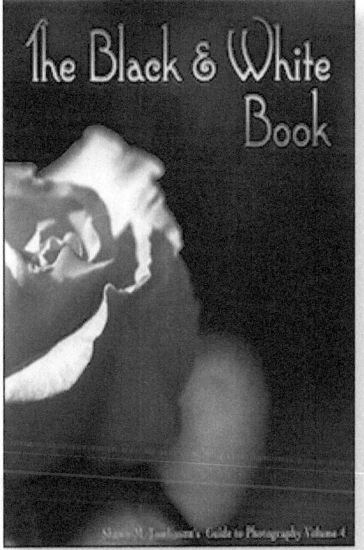

Shawn M. Tomlinson's Guide to Photography Series

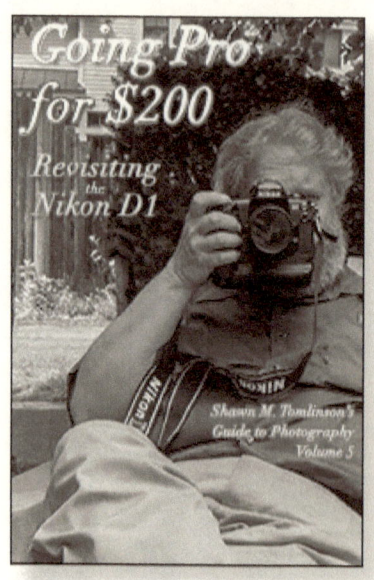

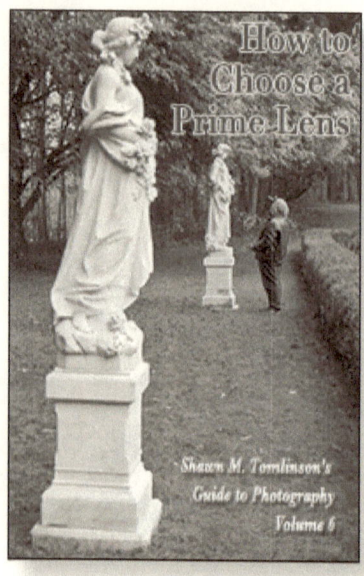

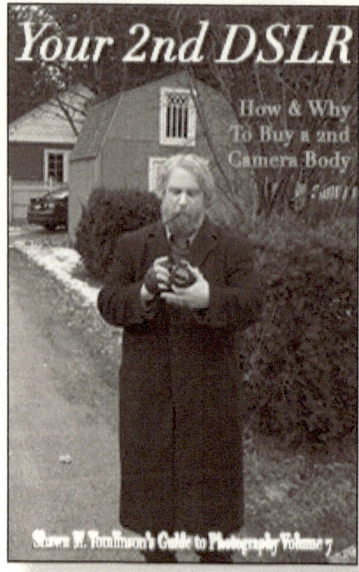

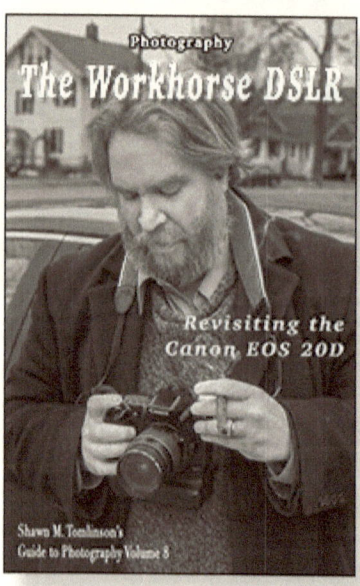

Shawn M. Tomlinson's Guide to Photography Series

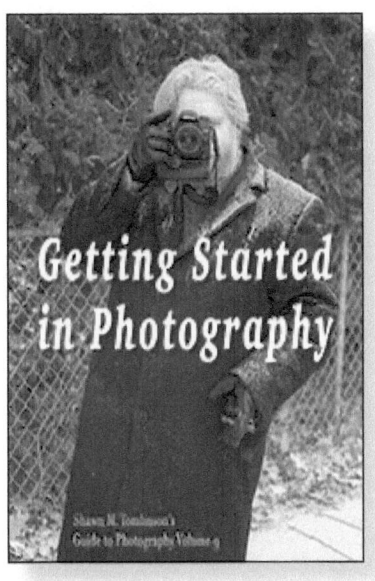

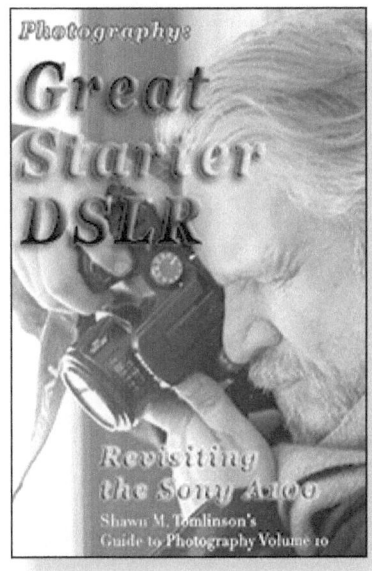

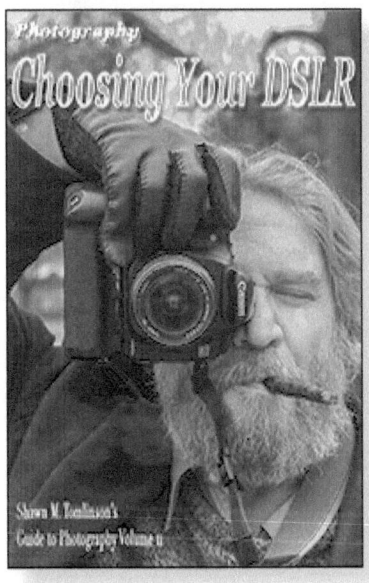

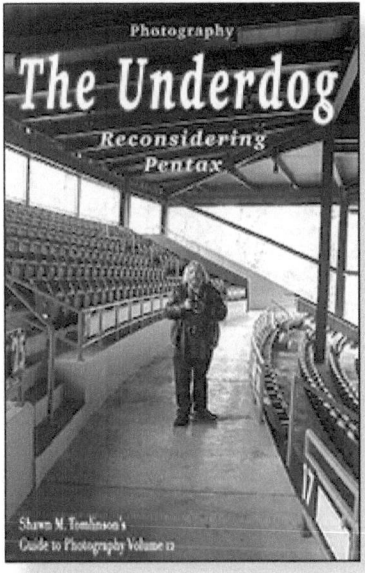

www.ingramcontent.com/pod-product-compliance
Lightning Source LLC
Chambersburg PA
CBHW022019170526
45157CB00003B/1290